Marriage: First Things First

God bless!

Grace Ketterman, M.D.

Marriage:
First Things
First

GRACE KETTERMAN, M.D.

BEACON HILL PRESS OF KANSAS CITY
Kansas City, Missouri

Cover design: Royce Ratcliff
Cover photo: Westlight
"How to Use This Book" and "Reflection and Action" sections: David J. Felter

10   9   8   7   6   5   4   3   2   1

Contents

How to Use This Book

There are many ways to use this text. Pastors and counselors will find this a useful resource for premarital counseling, marriage enrichment workshops, and sessions on family-living strategies. Teachers may use it in small groups or Sunday School class settings.

Many individuals or couples will find the insight and information they need to improve their marriages.

Dr. Ketterman believes families must nurture and sustain three characteristics if children are to grow up healthy: *warmth, acceptance,* and *structure.* This nurture happens best in the context of a healthy marriage. Working on your marriage is "putting first things first" with your family.

The goal of the end-of-chapter exercises is to involve readers in serious reflection and action. Dr. Ketterman identifies the values, beliefs, and actions that form the heart of good marriages. Just reading about them, however, is not enough. Each strategy, value, and belief holds transformative potential only as reflection is accompanied by action. The exercises are designed to help you engage in this process.

Introduction

A family must create a climate of warmth, acceptance, and structure if children are to grow up healthy. The essence of that climate is centered in a healthy marriage.

Many couples recognize early that their marriages are in trouble—or headed for stormy seas. Often they believe children will magically strengthen their relationship and still the tempests. Sadly, such magic rarely happens. Pregnancy and childbirth bring their own unique stresses, further testing marital relationships. Later, many of these troubled marriages are broken. All too often the children believe the breakup is their fault.

This truth may motivate you, as couples considering having a child, to take inventory.

- What is your marriage like?
- How firm is your commitment to one another?
- Do you have good communication skills?
- Can you disagree, debate, and decide on solutions graciously?
- Have you learned how to forgive?
- When crises (big or small) arise in your lives, do you cope with them redemptively, learning from them to be wiser and stronger?
- Do you each reserve some individuality in balancing intimacy?
- Have you discovered interests and activities to share?
- Do you discipline your time and arrange your priorities so you can enjoy such sharing?
- Have you developed an affirming, appreciative attitude instead of being critical and blaming?

- Finally, do you practice your faith in simple, practical ways daily in your home?

If you can answer all these questions positively, you have a healthy marriage. Chances are good that you will deal successfully with parenting functions. Even if the majority of your answers are affirmative, you'll be likely to make it. But if you've answered most of these questions negatively, you might be wise to wait before having a child.

Waiting, of course, is not enough if you are not working to make improvements in the meantime. If such work requires the help of a marriage and family counselor, find a good one. Healthy families do not simply happen. They are the masterpieces created through intense effort, solid guidance, and tenacity.

Every ounce of effort will be well worth your energy. At 68, when I experience my grandsons' assaults on me with hugs or when they gently say, "I love you," I know it was worth it. When I realize my adult children are my best friends, I know it was worth it. When my husband and I sit in an intimacy too deep for words, I know it.

This book is intended to help you take an inventory of your marriage. As you evaluate yourselves and where the strengths and weaknesses of your relationship are, you will be able to work on the issues you discover. We will explore 10 major categories vital in the development of a healthy marriage.

- Sexuality
- Jealousy
- Establishing priorities
- Spiritual bonding
- Activity sharing
- Effective communication
- Personality differences
- Balancing dependence with independence

- Developing personal character
- Sound commitment

Take the time to strengthen your weak spots if you find them. Revel in your strengths, and make them even more solid.

Find a balance between caution and overcaution. Don't wait for your marriage to be perfect before you have children. Few children would ever have been born if their parents waited for perfection. Any intimate relationship is in a constant state of dynamic change and growth. Your children will learn from your efforts, and even your mistakes, as they will from your successes.

As I look back on more than 40 years of married life, I can tell you there were tragic mistakes and almost unbearable pain at times. But strength has accumulated through righting the wrongs, exchanging forgiveness, and finding the courage to move forward.

I pray your mistakes will be few and your joys ever increasing. I hope for you, someday, a perspective as satisfying and rewarding as mine.

1

Sexual Intimacy

Barbara and Alan, back home from their honeymoon only a few weeks, were learning the importance of clear communication. They had made an exceptionally exciting sexual adjustment, glad they had waited until marriage for that experience.

After a harrowing day at work, Alan was exhausted—relieved to be at home, to sink into the soft new sofa and just relax. Shortly Barbara joined him, teasing, playfully seeking his attentions, expecting their usual passionate promenade to the bedroom.

After several minutes, Barbara realized Alan did not have the bedroom in mind. He patted her shoulder listlessly and then acted as if she weren't even there. She felt the clutch of rejection knotting in her stomach. What if her new husband was losing interest already? Perhaps she wasn't as good in bed as she had thought. She felt frightened and a little angry. Had Alan deceived her? They had had such a romantic honeymoon!

Meanwhile, Alan was even more troubled than his bride. Did he suffer from some strange malady? He certainly wasn't impotent—just tired and stressed. Unable to comprehend the situation, he began feeling irritated and impatient with Barbara. Surely it must be her fault! She was a bit careless in her grooming, and at times she talked too much. Why didn't she give him some space? Unable to define the problem, Alan pretended to fall asleep on the couch to avoid having to cope with it.

Barbara escaped to their bedroom and cried. Then she determined to accept the responsibility of taking action. Wiping her tears, she carefully applied some makeup. She returned to the sofa where Alan lay. In a gentle voice, she suggested they go out for dinner at a simple, quiet place they both liked.

Over their meal, Barbara and Alan talked—tentatively at first, then in earnest. Having time to think, and feeling safe with Barbara's tenderness, Alan owned his fears. He had grown up believing men were always more sexually aggressive than women. He admitted feeling powerless when he had no desire to respond to her.

Barbara, in turn, discussed her hurt and fear of rejection. She felt relieved to know Alan still loved her and was only exhausted.

Sexual intimacy pervades most of the basic concerns in marriage. It may be intense or diminished, but it is one vital means of communicating. Unless you both can talk about your interest or lack thereof, sex will become a battleground or a frightening specter instead of the warm bond of the intimacy you deserve.

You can imagine a different ending to this episode had the couple not talked. Even so early in their marriage, Barbara and Alan began to discover true intimacy—that of one hurt soul reaching out to the other for help—and finding it in understanding and acceptance.

Every day dozens of decisions must be made in every marriage. Many of them are individual ones—what you will wear, what you will eat, and when or if you will carry out household tasks. Other decisions need to be jointly made—how the money will be spent, where you will go for vacations, and which church you will attend.

How will you communicate in reaching all these decisions? One couple I know reached such an impasse and finally sought counseling. One of the first observations I made was this: When one spoke, the other seemed to be still, listening to the other's point of view. The responses each made, however, clearly revealed no real listening had taken place. When I asked Anne to repeat what Brent had just said, she was unable to do so. Brent, in turn, could clearly repeat what his wife had said, but he gave her ideas no respect.

Anne later admitted that her mind was focused completely on the point she was about to make. She really had not paid any attention to Brent's words, much less to his feelings.

Brent, who heard clearly, listened only so he could break down Anne's line of thinking. You can imagine how she reacted.

Instead of communicating, this couple was engaged in a power struggle—battling to the finish. Since neither was willing to change his or her habits, nor to give up fighting, the problems were not resolved. After several children and many painful years of such struggles, Brent and Anne divorced. I believe their divorce, along with many others, could have been avoided.

Ongoing disagreements, never fully resolved, seriously endanger enjoyable sexual intimacy. The arguments that result in insults from verbal abuse distance most couples promptly. What if Alan had begun to voice his mental criticisms of Barbara to explain away his own lethargy? She very likely would have found fault with him for leaving dirty socks and underwear on the floor. You can be almost certain each would have hugged the outside of their bed that night. The pain such hurtful comments inflicted would have created permanent scars. Over time, reconciliation takes place, but when too many incidents pile up, they become an impenetrable wall—right down the center of the bed.

Great sexual adjustments do not just happen—they take work. Let's look at some steps you can take to create an exciting sex life.

1. *Begin with attitude.* Do you see sexual intimacy as your *right?* If you feel it's your spouse's *duty* to give you sexual pleasure, you've defeated your relationship from the start. Reread Gen. 2. In simple terms, the Bible makes it clear that God created woman for joy and companionship with her husband. Sexual relations are intended for pleasure—fun and closeness—as well as for procreation. In fact, children are not even mentioned until later in the biblical account. Develop an attitude of mutuality about your sex lives. How can each most joyfully pleasure the other? Discuss ideas and techniques that enhance the pure fun of God's created gift of ultimate physical closeness.

2. *Resolve all conflicts promptly.* To avoid that regular clinging to the sides of the bed, stop fighting in the kitchen! When you do have disagreements, settle them promptly. Learn to disagree agreeably. We'll discuss this more in the chapter on communication.

3. *Express simple affection.* Many individuals have told me they hesitate to show any affection to their spouse for fear it will trigger prompt sexual demands. This should be changed. A warm embrace, gentle kiss, or playful tickling should not always prompt intercourse. When this expectation becomes a habit, one spouse is likely to recoil from all touching.

4. *Begin early to find broad-spectrum intimacy.* Some individuals desire and seem to need sexual intimacy much more frequently than others. Each couple should discuss the frequency of sexual relations in their marriage. Doing

so will be most successful if both persons work at the total concept of intimacy. One husband I know craves intellectual closeness. He bemoans his wife's inability or unwillingness to read and discuss great books or even current events with him. Another spouse loves nature, but she had to give up the dream of her husband's watching a sunset or wading in the ocean with her. Yet each spouse can explore the other's feelings and interests, developing total interpersonal intimacy. The more areas of interest you develop and share with each other, the more *true* intimacy you will know. Often, developing a wider scope of shared interests creates more meaningful sexual intimacy.

5. *Clean out old tapes.* Many people grow up with vague impressions taught by their parents' often unspoken attitudes. These concepts vary from believing sex is bad or dirty and that "men want only *one* thing" to the opposite extreme. Some believe it is their right to have sex on demand—and they demand often—making sexual slaves out of their spouses. Whatever your preconceived notions about sex are, set them aside to discover the truth. Renew your minds and beliefs from Scripture. The Bible compares the bride and bridegroom to Christ's unity with His Church. As a marriage partner, do you see your spouse in this glorious, even sacred, image?

If you are half of a couple who struggles with great differences in your desire for sex, deal with that problem.

Do not play the martyr. Making your spouse feel guilty or manipulating him or her to humor your demands causes major problems.

Do not stubbornly refuse to admit the spouse's frustration. When one is in the mood for sex and is even sexually aroused, it is a compliment to the partner. It may be painfully difficult to postpone sexual fulfillment. With some effort, see if you can gladly respond. You may be surprised to find that sexual desire is influenced by your mind-set.

Budget your time and energy. The one who craves sex more often can sublimate some of that energy by physical exercise or focusing on some good deeds for others. The partner who is less interested can grow in desire by thinking positively and creatively. How can your next episode of lovemaking be more romantic or creative? Candlelight and a full massage can help. So can a new time and place. Thinking imaginatively about the fun and good feelings you have had or believe you may have can help. Talk freely with your spouse about this.

Do not define your sexual prowess by frequency or intensity of orgasms. True sexuality means you are secure in your masculinity or femininity. You do not have to prove it by counting the number of encounters!

Total intimacy reminds me of the mystical ocean. Each wave is similar to the last yet is individually unique. Waves come with energy and often spectacular beauty.

As I watched this magnificent display of the Creator's power for the first time, I expected each wave to leave a treasury of seashells. That didn't happen. It took the imperceptible ebbing of the ponderous tides to produce the intriguing wealth of the sea's treasure.

Sexual joy is similar. Each experience can be magnificent in its waves of pure joy. But the real wealth of interpersonal intimacy comes only with the slow tides of the years.

When stress hits your marriage with its crashing storms, wait it out. It's tempting to want to leave the ship. In today's world, divorce is frighteningly easy—allowing people to evade their original commitment to one another. Escaping the waves, however, often means missing the treasure of the tide of life's seasons. Hold steady on the Rock that is safe. He will see you through those storms, building a masterpiece marriage!

Reflection and Action

Power struggles are often at the heart of communication disorders. The following exercises focus on improving a climate of intimacy.

1. Inventory those areas of shared interest:

Husband	Wife	Mutual
a.	a.	a.
b.	b.	b.
c.	c.	c.

2. Review the following Bible texts regarding marital intimacy and write a brief synopsis:

   a. Gen. 2

   b. Eph. 5:25ff.

   c. 1 Cor. 7:3-5

3. Discuss the issues, events, or circumstances that currently provide the most stress in your life.

   a.

   b.

   c.

4. Two couples were mentioned in the chapter. Barbara and Alan learned to communicate early on and their marriage flourished. Anne and Brent refused to communicate well—and divorced. What is your communication problem like? Write a strength, a weakness, and a goal.

2

Jealousy

"For jealousy is the rage of a man: therefore he will not spare in the day of vengeance. He will not regard any ransom; neither will he rest content, though thou givest many gifts" (Prov. 6:34-35).

After a long day on her feet as a saleslady, Diane returned home anticipating a chance to relax and enjoy some time alone with Jim. She hurried up the stairs to the bedroom, kicked off her shoes, and began to change clothes. Absentmindedly she flipped on the answering machine to retrieve the day's messages. What she heard there would change her life forever.

A man's voice, one Diane had never heard before, was shouting profanities at her out of the recorder. Jim, he accused, was having an affair with his wife. He ended the message by threatening to have Jim fired and slamming down the receiver.

Diane had always trusted her husband, but now she felt the horror of experiencing her first doubts about Jim. Could he have had an affair with this woman who worked on his floor? The 45 minutes until Diane heard Jim's car in the driveway seemed like an eternity. After a strained hello, Diane took Jim upstairs to play the tape, hoping and praying he would deny it all. Instead, the shame and guilt on Jim's face told the story. Jim admitted the truth. He had only wanted to be friendly and had no intention of having an affair. The woman was very attractive—even downright seductive. In a moment of weakness he had succumbed to her advances. The relationship was turbulent and short-lived. Jim was repentant, willing to own responsibility for his mistake.

In time, Diane forgave Jim. He repeatedly affirmed his love for her and his remorse over his actions. He vowed it would never happen again. She loved Jim and took their marriage vows seriously. Of course she would give him another chance! She tried never to bring up the event and disciplined herself to believe in his integrity once again.

Yet their life was never quite the same. When he hugged women friends at church or in their home, she inwardly recoiled. Could it happen again? She struggled against it but finally had to face it: she was jealous. The earlier event had not created the jealously, but it had certainly aroused it. For years Diane silently battled the terrible force of this painful feeling. There were other women who, she observed, held an unusual fascination for Jim.

Diane competed with them. She lost weight, changed her hairstyle, and invested in a new wardrobe. Nothing changed. In desperation, she sought counseling. Over time she learned these vital facts:

1. Her primary pain grew out of her deep inner insecurities. Diane saw herself as a "plain Jane" who would never be as glamorous as other women. She learned differently. It was a glorious day when she discovered that Jim was blessed to have her for a wife. She knew finally that she was a fine, valuable person. There was no longer a sense that another woman could outshine her inner beauty.

2. She learned that Jim was vulnerable to other women because of his insecurities. It made him feel "macho" to have women flirt with him. Yet he failed at times to set

clear boundaries with them. He was dangerously close to repeat affairs.

꘡3. Her watchfulness over Jim and his friendships had turned into nagging. She had become possessive of him in ways he could not handle. He experienced this as control or "mothering" and was driven away from Diane, whom he really did love.

Diane learned it would take time, but she vowed to overcome her jealousy and nagging. After some excruciating years, she did. The two finally made a healthy adjustment and, in fairy-tale fashion, *did* live happily!

This scenario has a reverse version. Dale caught his wife, Nan, in an inappropriate relationship with her boss. He, too, tried desperately to deny the truth. Nan was the one who felt so guilty that she sobbed out the truth.

Dale first railed against the man, supposedly a respected person in his field. He then raged at Nan, accusing and labeling her with degrading terms.

Finally Dale chose to look at himself. He realized that he had been neglecting his wife. He had taken her good qualities for granted and had forgotten the nice gifts he once had given her for no reason at all.

In spite of taking more than his share of the blame, Dale, too, struggled with insecurity and jealousy. With counseling, the couple hung together and mended their broken lives.

Jealousy may be learned from childhood and often has no basis in fact. Jed was a jealous husband. He knew his own father had cheated on his mother. He was a highly competitive child and throughout his teens became furious if he lost at games or failed to be at the top of his class in grades.

Jed married a lovely girl. She was bubbly and affectionate, friendly with everyone, men and women alike. Jed began to doubt her commitment to him. He would follow his wife when she went on errands, and if she stayed in any place too long, he would burn with jealous rage. Despite never finding her with another man, he became convinced that she was unfaithful.

Jed's accusations led to angry arguments, and his wife began to fear that he would abuse her. Eventually Jed *did* become abusive, and she felt she had to leave him to protect her life. Jed's early experiences left scars that distorted his perceptions.

Diane and Dale both experienced the tragic fallout of a spouse's unfaithfulness—the loss of an ideal and a dream. They each believed they had found the greatest mate and worked to build the best marriage possible. Each of them failed. Their mates were made of clay, highly breakable. And they did indeed break.

Any significant loss causes grief. And grief involves several well-defined stages. The first is denial. These people denied, at first, that *their* spouses could fall so low!

The next stage of grief is anger and blame. They felt angry at the spouse, the "other one," that one's spouse, and not least of all themselves. Had they taken too much blame, they would have given permission to their spouses to carry on—almost guilt-free. The balance in assigning responsibility to others, without blame, and assuming their own faults was not easy to find. Both experienced some guilt for their own inadequacies. They endured the sadness and pain of their losses. And at last, they reached the stage of resignation and felt the gradual healing that restored them.

Jed's jealousy, not based on fact, probably contained some of this grieving process also. But in his case, erroneous ideas and perceptions were at fault. He needed good psychotherapy to help him separate his past from the actual, here-and-now events.

There is another kind of jealousy we need to consider. It may be very difficult to understand, but it is most important to do so. This is the concept of godly jealousy.

God's chosen people, the Israelites, had a serious propensity to leave Him and to fall in love with heathen gods. Again and again, God allowed them to suffer the consequences of their unfaithfulness. But He always brought them back, sooner or later, to himself. In Exod. 20 we read of God's saying, "I the LORD thy God am a jealous God" (v. 5) and "Thou shalt have no other gods before me" (v. 3).

In a healthy marriage there needs to be this kind of jealousy! Good jealousy says, "I know we belong together. I'm the best for you, as you are for me. If I see you wandering astray—where I know you and I both are in danger of pain—I will call you back! I can't force you to return at once, just as God didn't compel His people to come back immediately. But I will wait, pray, and do whatever I can to woo you back."

You can see this type of jealousy comes from strength, commitment, and love. It has no insecurity or fear about oneself. Many marriages could be not only saved but enriched as well by such a stand.

Perhaps you are jealous of your spouse. There are some vital actions for you to consider:

\ 1. Is the problem yours, like Jed's, or is the problem your spouse's, like Diane's? The answer to this question demands painful honesty. You may need to ask a trustworthy friend if he or she has seen a sign of straying in your spouse. If you find no evidence of such, work on your mind. Clarify your thinking, separate the past from now, and make a repeated, conscious choice to trust your spouse until undeniable evidence is found. Sooner or later such evidence will turn up if it's there.

\ 2. If your spouse has betrayed you, you must confront the issue, or you will become an enabler. How to pull off such a confrontation successfully, of course, is the challenge. It's important to start with facts you can support with evidence. Avoid opinions and idle gossip. Keep an open mind—perhaps your information is in error. Watch for signs of deception—nervousness and evasiveness are usually important signs. Give your spouse time to level with you; sudden ultimatums or impulsive actions often result in regrets.

3. Have a person handy to consult as an adviser: someone who will not take sides with either of you and who can objectively help both of you. Listen to this person's impressions and take time to think about that point of view.

4. Avoid sending ultimatums to your spouse. This will only create defensiveness and rebellion. But do formulate some clear definitions of what you can live with, how long you can wait for change, and even how you will know such a change is genuine.

5. Be prepared for a separation, but do not choose such action lightly.

6. I strongly urge both spouses to seek counseling, individually and as a couple, to work out problems whenever possible.

You can see, if you plan to have children, how crucially important it is that you overcome jealousy. The danger it implicates to any degree of security as a family is extremely high. It is both unwise and unfair to choose to bring a child into such a shaky situation. The old supposition that a child will strengthen a failing marriage is erroneous.

If you happen to conceive a child during a time of such stress, let that motivate you to work through your problems. Do not choose abortion as the easy way out. With wise professional help, the weak areas of most marriages can be strengthened, and the marriage can become healthy. Success will depend on forgiving, forgetting, and moving forward, committed to the rest or your lives.

Jealousy can be overcome; its grief can be healed. Personal and marital health can be encouraged and achieved. And it must be done if you are to be really ready to have a child.

If you already have a child when this tragic feeling invades your hearts, get help at once. Children do not deserve to be damaged emotionally by the separation of their parents. Children are a part of each parent—they love both and cannot understand the tension that jealousy creates. Few issues dictate as authoritatively as having a child. Work it out! Solve the problems. Negotiate and give in where possible. If both of you put your child's needs ahead of your petty selfishness, you can have not just a bearable but a truly *great* marriage.

Reflection and Action

Dr. Ketterman suggests that jealousy may often be the result of personal insecurity, inappropriate patterns of parenting, or negative experiences during childhood involving the behavior of a parent.

1. If you have had a parent who was unfaithful in marriage, examine your feelings about that situation. Are these feelings interfering with your relationship with your spouse?

2. What constructive methods, taken from Ketterman's example of godly jealously, should be used in dealing with a spouse tempted to stray?

   a.

   b.

   c.

3. What is an *enabler?* In what way does Ketterman use this term?

4. What is the difference between an ultimatum and clearly defined expectations concerning the marriage relationship, and when should this strategy be employed?

5. How do children affect the urgency for solving marital problems?

3

Prioritizing

Years ago, after I had presented a seminar on Christian parenting, a sad-faced mother confronted me. She had obviously traveled rough roads in life, and her face depicted some of the road map. Her startling problem rested in the fact that her three grown sons were homosexuals. She could find none of the acceptance of her situation that has become more common today, and her heart was breaking. In the midst of her personal anguish, Beth had laboriously found some of the reasons for her sons' lifestyle.

She and her husband were dedicated to their fine church. Both of them gave generously of time and money to support it. Her husband, however, gave beyond the usual commitment.

At least six nights a week and much of the weekend, this devoted man was at his church. He served on boards and committees, helped with cleaning and repairs, and never missed a service. He rarely found time for their three growing boys except to be sure they were proper and well-behaved.

To Beth was relegated the task of training and entertaining these robust sons. She didn't know how to play ball, and her husband didn't want them out with the rowdy kids in the neighborhood. She couldn't stand the idea of putting worms on a fishing hook, much less taking off a wriggling, scaly fish. All she knew how to do was cook and bake, clean and sew, crochet and knit. These things she carefully taught her well-loved sons.

Beth grieved as she understood that her husband's priorities had been wrong—tragically so. His rigid expectations, absence from home (even for a good cause), and failure to show love and companionship created a chasm between him and his sons. They had no masculine role model—so they identified with their loving, feminine mother.

Let me tell you another tragically true story about a man named Vernon. This man had grown up in poverty, but he worked his way to a college degree. He did well in business and learned how to make money—lots of it. It felt much better to Vernon to be wealthy than poor. In fact, he fast discovered he could never have enough money.

Traveling was necessary in Vernon's business. Many Sunday evenings he would say to his son, Greg, "Son, I'll be at the American Hotel in New York this week. Be sure to call me there if you need anything! And here's $50.00 to take care of you while I'm gone!" Vernon loved Greg. He was proud of his developing physique and charm. Someday they'd have time together!

Greg soon learned how to invest his money. It was easy to parlay that $50.00 into several hundred dollars by selling drugs. And his own loneliness was relieved by inhaling the toxins of those he didn't sell. Greg learned his absentee father would lovingly rescue him from all consequences of his illegal activities. Dad paid for his college tuition year after year only to grieve that Greg never got a credit, let alone a diploma.

Finally, Vernon retired, hoping he and Greg could do a little fishing. Maybe then he'd give up those drugs. But instead, Greg went to prison. His "pals" had turned against him and had reported his illegal activities. This time even Dad could not rescue him.

The disordered priorities of these men damaged their children for life. But consider also the pain of their spouses.

In spite of her best efforts to raise good Christian sons, Beth saw her dreams rust and her labors fall short. Her homosexual sons lived life contrary to biblical teaching. Though it was most difficult for her to reveal it, Beth admitted that she was angry at her husband. He had failed her as well as their sons. And now it was too late. How could she ever forgive him?

Vernon's wife, Lana, saw his neglect of Greg, but she also felt neglected. She had no one with whom to share her joys *or* sorrows. She took advantage of his money and tried to find solace in the things it bought. It was finally in Greg that she found companionship. He was willing to listen to her and even felt some significance in her confidences and seeking his advice. In turn, of course, Greg took advantage of her need for him to gain freedom beyond his capacity to handle.

It is not difficult to understand these two men and their countless clones. One had an intense need to prove himself to be a good, godly man, vital to his church. Who could fault him? Only those entrusted to his care—his wife and three sons.

And who, growing up in difficult economic times, would not quickly identify with Vernon? The apparent magic of trading poverty for riches appeals to many. Furthermore, his wife seemed to be faring well. She sparkled at his company's social events and was always there for him emotionally. He didn't even realize that she had resorted to displacing him with her son. Their marriage was a hollow, glittering shell.

Sometimes the scenario plays out in reverse. Penney, for instance, was elated to learn she was pregnant. Nine months later, her joy seemed complete when she gave birth to a perfect little girl. Her life became melded with that of her daughter. Every tooth she grew and each step she walked became events to Penney.

It was months before she even realized that her husband was gone more than usual. Phil treated her with respect, and together they functioned in their busy community activities. But if he even mentioned that he missed her, Penney would kiss him lightly, tousle his hair, and run off with her charming child. Phil tried to join them, but somehow he felt he could never break into their circle. He was too proud and kind to compete with his child for the attention of his wife. After 30 lonely years, Phil quietly filed for a divorce. A marriage was over.

These disguised, true stories are depictions of marriages gone awry later in life. But be certain of one fact—the taproots of these ugly weeds that choked the life out of these marriages began on the wedding day and even before. The priorities of these individuals were wrong. You see, even putting mothering ahead of your marriage is a grave and fatal mistake.

How does one sort through the values inherent in life and find the essential elements? How, early in marriage, can you plan your lives so you will not risk the unhappiness and separation these couples experienced?

You will note that Vernon brought to his marriage insecurities relating to his impoverished youth. Due to the anxiety of those years, he had a deep need to build financial security, though he never really discovered what that security was a substitute for. To avoid making Vernon's mistake, you must resolve the hurts and losses of the past. This will entail a grieving process. Grieving through your past can set you free to see the present clearly and enables you to make wise choices.

Let's take time to review the stages of grief briefly. First there is denial. In decades of working with troubled people, I have learned that accepting loss is one of the most painfully difficult challenges they face. The loss of dreams, the awareness that life did not measure up to their anticipations is too much—so they deny that loss or disappointment as long as possible.

When attempts at denial fail, people become angry and look for someone to blame. Vernon was angry at his father, who drank too much. Phil was silently furious at the wife who displaced him with their child. Possibly you, too, have some resentments or outright anger at the trials life has dealt you. You must face the fact and overcome the anger if you are ever to overcome your grief.

During or after the anger stage, you will enter the period of suffering. The pain, helplessness, and sense of injustice will hit you broadside. This feels like depression, but it is not the same, because you can identify the source of your pain. It's just that it's too late, many times, to correct the mistakes.

If you are not careful, you can bury yourself or your spouse in helpless remorse and hopeless guilt. You can spend the rest of your life wallowing in the "if onlys." I call such feelings of endless guilt and the self-pity that accompanies them "detours of grief." Be careful to avoid these bumpy roads. Seek God's forgiveness and that of those you have hurt. And, most difficult but absolutely essential, forgive yourself! Apologize if you can. Make explanations, but avoid being defensive. When you have made everything as right as you can, put the mistakes behind you and press forward. God knew all of us would need forgiveness and redemption, so He sent Christ to die for us, to pay the price for our wrongs so we can be free. Follow His plan.

It's freeing to find deliverance from guilt over past sins. It's even more wonderful to learn how to avoid repeating those mistakes and move into a brand-new future. How can you reorder your priorities to insure a healthy marriage? Here are some useful ideas:

1. *Take care of yourself!* Sound selfish? But think about the results of failing to do that. You will become drained and depressed—burned out. In such a condition you are not very useful to others.

On every plane trip a flight attendant explains to the passengers what to do in case of an emergency. In the event of a sudden drop in cabin pressure, he or she states, a yellow mask will drop in front of each passenger. We are carefully instructed to place the mask over our nose and mouth and breathe normally. We are strongly cautioned, if traveling with a child, to place our own masks on first and *then* to help the child. Sound selfish? Sure! But if the adult loses consciousness, the child will be unattended and will also faint. We must attend to our own needs and have a reservoir on which to draw if we ever hope to serve others.

2. *Be a partner to your spouse.* Valuing a partnership in marriage can avoid endlessly destructive hurts and power struggles. Think about what partners do:

a. They share risks and expenses.

b. They discuss ideas and needs, coming up with wise decisions after resolving differences.

c. They encourage and support each other as well as share concerns and losses.

d. They enjoy the winnings of profit.

There are many Christian leaders who advocate a hierarchy in godly families. They quote the many scriptures about wives being submissive to husbands. It is interesting to contemplate that women often find it easier to give in on many issues, thus keeping peace in the family. But when men use these words to justify becoming tyrants, it causes major trouble. It seems clear that God created Eve to be a helpmate (a partner) with Adam. The Scriptures beautifully state that men are to love their wives as Christ loved His Church—even to the death.

When both husband and wife respect each other,

think clearly, and stick with "What's best and wisest for both of us?" decisions and priorities will be established easily. Without such a plan, there will be rough roads ahead.

3. *Communicate effectively.* One husband admitted that he listened very well during arguments with his wife—in order to out-argue her. Good communication demands three skills:

a. *Learning to speak clearly the concepts of the mind.* Confused thinking and talking often make effective communication impossible. Take time to contemplate until you know what you believe, and then state your ideas concisely as well as clearly.

b. *Listening with an open mind—and heart.* How few people there are who practice this skill! Yet without it they will miss the core feelings that prompt the partner's points of view. Don't make the mistake of the husband who listened only in order to win.

c. *Understanding body language.* Most people are raised to believe that certain feelings and thoughts are wrong or sinful. For example, they may believe anger is totally unacceptable. They learn to speak in terms that deny the anger they may understandably feel. Looking at their eyes and clenched fists, however, one can clearly detect the rage inside. By stating gently, "Sam, I know you believe anger to be a sin, but I see you looking pretty mad; it's OK with me for you to feel anger—just tell me about it," you may defuse the anger and easily resolve the issue. Just imagine how safe Sam would feel with such understanding.

4. *Find mutually enjoyable activities.* During dating days, both partners focus on exciting things to do in a time together. After marriage, the demands on time and energy

consume each one so that fun gets excluded. Even the joyful intimacy of sex can become routine and lose its luster.

A healthy marriage must include the careful guarding of time for having fun together. Many couples forget what they once enjoyed and can actually find *no* shared interests anymore. Don't let that happen to you! Continue to explore new activities involving both work and play. Planting a garden, hiking, window-shopping, playing a new game, or sharing the ideas gleaned in reading a book or magazine may bond you more closely with one another. You must be honest with your spouse—don't try to act as though you love an activity just to please him or her! Don't deceive each other or yourself. Keep exploring until you find the activities you both *really* enjoy!

You will have a constant struggle to find time for these activities. Win that struggle at all costs if you want to build a healthy marriage!

5. *Be committed.* Recently I talked with a friend whose husband becomes very angry over certain issues. Rarely does he finish one of his tirades without yelling, "I don't know why I ever married you! I would have been so much happier if I'd married Carol—at least she had a brain!"

This fantasy that depicts how life *might* have been with a different person is a very risky approach. While Carol might have been more clear-thinking, she very well may have been domineering and cold. Unless your marriage is irreparably destroyed, make your commitment firm. Resist those temptations to dream of escaping, and spend your energy conceiving ways to make it wonderful!

6. *Make your faith the top priority.* Several researchers have found that practicing spiritual beliefs together has been found to be the top ingredient of all healthy families. As Christians, you have an unparalleled resource for making a strong marriage through Jesus Christ. He is your ef-

fective Mediator, your source of love, and the unerring wisdom you need. His power will enable you to succeed. I strongly urge you to find comfortable ways to talk, study, and pray about your life in Christ. Be careful to avoid using this part of your lives to criticize or put down your partner! It's very tempting to "sic" God on your spouse to "get him!" or her!

ᐟ 7. *Be prepared to postpone your present pleasure for the future good of your spouse and your marriage.* This definition of maturity is really crucial in defining and arranging your priorities. The way you spend money, accomplish daily tasks, and reach family goals rests on how well you master this skill. When both of you can practice this discipline, you will have mastered one of the most vital arts in life as well as in marriage.

Prioritizing demands constant awareness. It takes self-discipline and unselfishness. It requires ongoing assessment of the needs and goals of each family member. And it won't work unless you are willing to lose yourself in the good of all through the power of God. The great news is that He is always waiting for you to ask.

Reflection and Action

1. In Dr. Ketterman's first two illustrations of disordered priorities, what struck you as the critical element common to the persons involved?

2. Insecurity appears to be a contributing cause of disordered priorities in some people's lives.

   a. List Vernon's insecurities:

   b. List Beth's husband's insecurities:

3. Is one aware of the grief caused by an inner sense of loss?

4. How would the denials of Beth's husband have sounded to him? If you were his counselor, how would you have described the symptoms of his grief? What would you have said or recommended to him that would help him see through to the presence of denial in his life?

5. Ketterman makes a subtle statement about the difference between anger and depression. Did you catch it?

6. List three things you've recently given permission to yourself to do, that were just for you:

   a.

   b.

   c.

7. Review the three skills of good communication. List them here, using behavioral examples:

   a.

   b.

   c.

4

Spiritual Bonding

It seems to me there are few areas of life in which couples have more difficulty than in their spiritual bonding. This is true even when both come from the same denominational background, but it may be nearly impossible when each spouse comes from a different denomination.

Eugene grew up in a mainline church and had always been active in youth groups and attended church regularly. His new wife, Gwen, came from a smaller denomination and was steeped in its somewhat more conservative beliefs and traditions.

Where they attended did not matter a great deal to Eugene, so they joined Gwen's church after their wedding. Both became involved in the many functions of church life. Over time, however, it became clear that Eugene did not take these activities too seriously. He believed all the basics and certainly knew his salvation depended on faith in Christ. In spite of this commitment, the depth of the spiritual sharing between him and Gwen was clearly shallow. She began to yearn for a more genuine sharing of deeper spiritual concerns and growth. Eugene felt he was far ahead of most men he knew and couldn't comprehend her concern.

After nearly four decades of working with families

both professionally and through church seminars and teaching, I have recognized this problem in infinite variations. What happens between many couples is too often self-defeating. The yearned-for spiritual compatibility is lost in competition! Before either realizes it, such couples find themselves in power struggles. Someone inevitably loses.

Lucille grew up in a family where daily prayer and Bible reading were essential. At times, this ritual had seemed tedious to her, but later she understood its power in her spiritual development. She wanted to recapture the values of family worship in her new marriage.

Such a practice was new to her husband, and while he mentally acquiesced to the custom, Lucille soon faced the facts. His heart was not in it; he began to make excuses, and soon the family devotions became rare, then nonexistent.

Later, when their four children were born, Lucille struggled alone to build a family altar. But the lack of her husband's involvement left it a weaker structure than it should have been. The children silently wondered why Daddy never had time to share their devotions.

The power of prayer is immeasurable in the fight of good against evil. And the eternal wisdom of God's Word is vital in a Christian's growth and maturity. Satan and his hosts fight against God himself by making family devotions difficult or seemingly impossible.

How Can You Do It?

Let's think together of some ways you can win this struggle and both establish and keep your spiritual wellness at a high level.

1. *Make up your minds!* It is not enough to say to each other, "We really *must* start sharing devotions!" Nor is it likely to insure success if you say, "After Pastor's ser-

mon, I can see that we *have* to begin family prayers soon."
The "musts," "shoulds," "have tos," and "soons" all too
commonly are words of postponement. They relieve the
pain of a pricked conscience, but they are almost certainly
indicators that action will not follow. You must make a
definite decision together.

2. *Establish a clearly defined plan.* Carefully review
your schedules and the already structured demands on
your times. Consider when you are least fatigued, when
the interruptions are least likely, and when you can with
reasonably regularity get together.

As you work out your plan, consider these time possibilities: before or after a meal such as breakfast (if you are
morning people) or dinner (if you're not); think about a
format such as reading through the Psalms or studying a
New Testament Epistle; and consider adding a time-honored hymn or the writings of some of God's special saints.
There are many daily devotional books and periodicals
that can guide you as you adapt them to your own original
format.

3. *Think honestly about what events or attitudes could
sabotage your plan.* We all understand that to be fore-
warned is to be forearmed. But few of us are prepared for
the subtle seduction away from God's best by some very
good causes. What would you do, for example, if a friend
called just as you began to read your devotional material
and really *needed* to discuss a family problem? It's extremely tempting to believe that giving up your sacred time
would be the best, even the unselfish thing to do.

Such a reason for giving up your family devotions can
lead to giving up the whole program. Make an appoint-
ment to call your friend back and assure your caring about
any distress. My own parents demonstrated the vital importance of our family prayers. In the coldest of Midwest-
ern winters and busiest of summer harvests, our entire

family met every morning for our family worship. Those simple prayers for our safety and for God's miraculous provisions for our sometimes desperate needs provided me then and now with the certainty of His power.

Today's complexities make it far more difficult to keep any sort of regularity in life. On the other hand, my husband often reminds me that truly emergency calls have been extremely rare in our 40 years together. So I would urge you to turn on your telephone answering machine and prevent the tyranny of electronic gadgets from interfering with this priceless time together.

Perhaps one of the most common saboteurs of your devotional life is your own mind. How easy it is to think about the day past, the hours ahead, or the many duties that face you! Some remedies for this include thinking and talking through your day and making a specific plan for the tasks that await you. Eventually, you will simply have to take captive all those uncontrolled and hidden intruders by careful self-discipline.

4. *Develop a contingency plan for every possible saboteur.* Such plans are already listed for the examples above. You will discover countless other distractions that will endanger your devotional time. As each emerges, think about the best possible answer to it, and put that answer to work.

The degree of your commitment to a family worship time will measure its success. Do you honestly believe in its value, and are you determined to follow through?

Personal Devotions Too?

As important as sharing devotions is in spiritual bonding, this is not a substitute for a private quiet time with God. Your own time to learn to relate intimately with the Heavenly Father is vital to your spiritual growth.

There is, however, at least one warning we should

heed—it is possible to become a spiritual "snob"! In fact, you probably know people who are exactly that. They are the ones whose talk is full of special messages direct from God. They manage just to let it slip that they have spent so many minutes in prayer and that they have certainly remembered you and your last trial with your spouse. You worry a bit at such a statement and whether this individual has shared the confidence with another person as well as with God.

Now this may seem at first a bit cynical, but it isn't. The most deeply spiritual people with the greatest devotional lives are usually fairly quiet about it. They live out God's love and power in a quietly humble way that speaks more loudly than sermons. A saint of old had admonished succinctly, "Preach Christ! And if you *must,* use words!"

You can readily see that if your spiritual life and growth outstrip your spouse's, a barrier will develop, rather than a bond. If you suspect such a thing is happening, seek special guidance from the Lord. God will guide you so that your spiritual life will not be stunted, and also so that you will not grow away from each other.

Always be alert for any destructive degree of competition. Healthy rivalry spurs you on in the growth process. That which is not healthy puts down and denigrates the other; this must be avoided at all costs.

Throughout life there is a constant search for proper balance. Being open and honest with each other is vital to a healthy marriage. But the balance for openness is the ability to have periods of comfortable silence. In achieving personal spiritual maturity, without putting down your mate, you may well need the skill of studied quietness.

Other Resources for Spiritual Bonding

Form friendships with spiritually mature people. It is not easy for couples to find other couples with whom they are compatible. By further restricting your search to a truly spiritually mature and healthy other couple, you may have a challenge. Look, listen, and pray for guidance. In time, you'll find a couple with whom you're compatible. It may be an older couple in your church or a young couple in your neighborhood.

When you find such spiritual mentors, don't wear them out. Find some areas in which you can enrich their lives as they enhance yours.

Attend church services regularly. Once again, you must establish balances and boundaries. At one time I found myself spending more than 20 nights a month in church responsibilities. There were services at least twice a week, home visitation, board and committee meetings, and women's activities. I soon learned that my family suffered in the good service to my church.

Seek the guidance of your pastor. Ask him or her to help you select the activities in your church that will best meet your needs. Look equally for the ways you can be of use to your church. Then limit your time to those areas in which you are led to participate.

Watch TV selectively. Few things in life are more seductive or more addictive than television. Sportscasts alone can separate you as a couple and lead to resentment or guilt. Yet what is more wholesome than a top-notch sporting event?

It may be tempting to abandon your husband to his sports and go shopping or find activities in a remote area of your home. Before you know it, you can become strangers in your own bedroom as well as in your spiritual sanctuary.

Disciplining your time in front of the TV takes immense determination and self-control. Select the programs you both enjoy, and limit the number you watch to prevent the addiction they can soon become.

In choosing entertainment, I recommend good, wholesome secular programs as well as the fine Christian ones that are available in most areas. You live in a world that is growing ever more pagan. You need to recognize good from evil and to distinguish the best from the good. Observe critically, discuss ideas together, and you will find you are growing in your sense of discernment. Avoid being judgmental of each other's ideas.

ᵕ *Look around you.* In most communities there are Christian events such as concerts and seminars. No one denomination can afford all these beneficial opportunities. Avail yourselves of some of these. Once again, practice discernment. Be sure to seek God's guidance and wisdom to avoid chasing every interesting teaching that comes along.

ᵕ *Learn to read, listen, and think.* It is widely known that the average American reads only on the sixth grade level. The soporific impact of TV with its inducement to passive listening has robbed us of the need to think deeply. People tend to react emotionally to both preachers and politicians. It's urgently important that couples think together. Discuss not just things and people but values and ideas as well. The Bible clearly tells us the Holy Spirit is the Spirit of truth. Stay dependent on Him, and He will clarify truth from deception for you.

ᵕ *Find God the Creator.* In spite of the ways people pollute and litter our land, there are many places where one can still see the beauty of God's world. Without leaving your own neighborhood, be attuned to the One who painted the magnificence of rainbows, the incomparable call of the cardinal, or the innocent, trusting gaze of baby animals. Don't lose your sense of awe and wonder; share it with your spouse and learn the areas of life that inspire his or her heart similarly.

When cut-throat competition in your jobs gets to you, go for a walk. Let the bits and pieces of yet-unspoiled loveliness invade your heart and senses. You will rediscover that His power eventually will make things right for you.

Look for traces of the Holy Spirit in those who walk in Him. It is easier for many people to be critical of others instead of finding their assets. Don't let that critical spirit control your mind. Work hard to develop an affirming, appreciative attitude. Such a spirit will work wonders in your marriage and especially in your spiritual bonding.

What If He or She Won't Join Me?

One of the saddest questions I am asked by a spouse is this one: "My husband (or wife) just isn't interested in spiritual things—what can I do?" The question burns even more deeply into my awareness when there are children. How can a little child reconcile the differences between a believing parent and a spiritually lukewarm or cold one? It is so important to settle your spiritual differences and find some degree of unity before you have a child!

If you have an unbelieving spouse and are looking for guidance, read 1 Cor. 7, noticing especially verse 14. Perhaps through your steadfast love for God and your spouse, you may be an instrument by which your partner comes to know the Lord.

Avoid preaching at or nagging your spouse. Gently, sincerely live out your own faith. Let your life be an example of the salt people described in Matt. 5:13—the ingredient that serves as an appetizer for those who lack it.

The great truth is this: your spouse's lack of spiritual life need not hinder the growth of the fruit of the Spirit in you! When God's love, joy, peace, patience, kindness, goodness, faithfulness, gentleness, and self-control are evident in your life, few people can resist the craving for them in their lives (see Gal. 5:22). In addition, you will become increasingly happy yourself. You may think of this as a secret between you and the Father.

If your husband or wife just won't join you in your family devotions, doesn't like nature, and complains about most sermons, there are only a few choices.

1. You can feel sorry for yourself and play the martyr for your spouse—an almost certain path to mutual misery.

2. You can give up your own spiritual walk with God and end up living far away from God, unable to help your spouse or yourself to a great Christian life.

3. You can find the good aspects of your spouse and enjoy and encourage him or her. Meanwhile, you can allow Jesus Christ to grow the fruit of His Spirit in you, quietly, gently reveling in them, letting them draw your spouse (and others) to crave the knowledge of God themselves.

Reflection and Action

1. List at least two reasons why companions from differing religious traditions or backgrounds find it difficult to achieve spiritual bonding:

   a.

   b.

   c.

2. Ketterman speaks of *deciding, defining,* and *predicting* as strategies useful in developing spiritual bonding. Use these to plan your own strategy for facilitating or enhancing spiritual bonding with your spouse:

   a. We decide to _____ to help us achieve spiritual bonding.

   b. We define our goals or expectations in the following terms: _____, _____, _____.

   c. We predict these items or elements will pose interference to this process: _____

   _____

3. Describe your own personal devotional habits.

4. Use the following to discover and identify additional resources for spiritual bonding:

   a. Name of a desirable spiritual mentor: _____
   _____

   b. Public worship opportunities to which I commit: _____
   _____

   c. TV and entertainment practices I want to alter or change: _____

   d. Personal reading / reflection goals I would like to incorporate: _____

5

Sharing Activities

When Heather and Dave began dating, they found the days too short! There were so many things to do—hikes to take, picnics to plan, sports events to cheer, concerts to hear, friends to share, games to play, and often a silent, blazing sunset to see—while just holding hands! But incredibly, here they were, a brief six months into their marriage, and both of them were painfully, even frighteningly, aware of feeling bored. In fact, at times they sensed a growing awareness of resentment toward each other.

One Saturday morning Dave woke up ready for one of their old, day-long bike hikes. What a great idea! But Heather failed to see the greatness as she viewed a mountain of laundry, a dirty house, an unkempt lawn, and grocery shopping to do before Monday's rat-race began. Angrily she yelled, "Dave, all you want is your own selfish fun! How can we be gone all day when there's so much work to do? You never consider my responsibilities, but you can always find time for *your* plans!"

Crestfallen, Dave, who liked peace at all costs, apologized and they stayed home. Sullenly and with a twinge of underlying guilt, both worked so hard they collapsed into bed early—and slept on the edges of their bed. How soon the pleasures and romance of dating can be lost in the duties of being conscientious householders!

Yet there are some easy and successful solutions for problems like Dave and Heather experienced. Here are some ideas that would have saved their day and bonded them more closely:

1. *They could have negotiated.* For example, they could have whizzed through some housecleaning and a load or two of laundry, arranged a time to catch up on the yard work, and then they could have hiked for the rest of the day. Imagine returning after a quick stop at the grocery store to a cozy, intimate evening together.

2. *They could have planned ahead.* Keeping household tasks done on a daily, scheduled basis would have prevented the stack-up that made Heather feel such despair. Or planning an activity ahead of time could allow for a bit of catch-up before the weekend. It's true, however, that impulsive, spontaneous activities once in a while create memories that nothing else can match!

3. *They could have graciously generated an alternate plan.* Dave, for example, seeing the reality of Heather's perspective and knowing her need to have household jobs done properly, could have said, "Honey, I guess I've still got a lot to learn about being a husband. I really don't help you very much. Let's postpone the hike until next Saturday. Today, you teach me how to help you the best, and this week we'll do it together!" Few wives could stay miffed with such an offer. They could have had a good day, a great week, and a more cemented relationship.

4. *They could have gone biking for several hours and then come home to deal with the most necessary tasks.* The one problem with this plan could be the fatigue a bike trip causes. They may have failed to do the jobs and felt too stressed over the work.

You may have some of your own ideas about creative solutions. The big point is this—don't settle for bad, mad, or hurt feelings. Think lovingly, empathetically, and creatively. You can always find an answer to the demands of life that will crowd out fun.

Don't forget, by the way: sharing activities doesn't always mean playing together. *Working* together can also be fun.

Planning Together

Bruce, just home from his honeymoon, was intent on becoming a blue-ribbon husband. He and his bride were unpacking their wedding gifts and arranging their new apartment. Enthusiastically, he began to place objects and pictures in all the wrong places. Helen, his wife, tried tactfully to suggest other possible arrangements, but being a strongly opinionated person, he defended his ideas. Before long Helen was in tears, and Bruce was bewildered.

In all successful teams, there are strengths and weaknesses unique to each member. A healthy marriage is really a team. If each partner will define what he or she is good at and admit that in other areas he or she is not so strong, the couple can create a successful division of basic categories of responsibilities.

He may be great at cooking, and she may have the skills of a master gardener, so be careful to avoid trite old "shoulds" and "oughts." Traditionally, he should do all the mechanical jobs. But some "hes" are all thumbs and create more havoc than repairs. She, on the other hand, may have mastered some fine skills in this department. Each needs to avoid putting down the other for not measuring up to preconceived notions about job descriptions.

Once the areas of strengths and weaknesses are defined, the household tasks need to be listed under the big categories. Shopping, decorating, upkeep, and repairs can hardly be written in too much detail.

Each one will help the marriage if a major point is clarified early on. Do you like to do your work independently? Or do you like to have help? From driving nails to folding towels, there are advantages to working alone *and* together. It's a matter of personality and habits. When I'm getting a big holiday meal ready, I often need to be alone in my kitchen. Even the most eager helper may distract and confuse me. At other points, however, I need lots of help in setting tables, pouring beverages, and greeting guests. Let each other know your preferences, and be clear that your needs are just that—not an attempt either to control or to reject the other.

In sharing work activities, there is another major danger. Each partner enters marriage with different standards for quality performance. Few interactions will cause more damage than repeated criticisms of his or her work. I heard one wife find fault with at least 10 areas in which her husband tried to help and please her. The clothes were not sorted properly, the dishes were misplaced in the dishwasher, there were edges of dust or dirt if he vacuumed, and the bathroom sink sometimes had water spots on it. No wonder he found work that increasingly kept him away and other friends who affirmed him. Men, we all know, can be just as critical, so this problem is not gender-limited.

What can you do, then, if the quality of your spouse's work is clearly inadequate?

1. *You may lower your standards.* For minor variations, I recommend this approach. Perfectionism is toxic, and you may carry it so far that your mate gives up ever meriting your much-needed approval.

2. *For standards that put your social lives and household safety at risk, however, you may need to communicate.* Writing out together some standards and methods may work. Pointing out someone else's approach, though risky, may be a teaching mode. Offering help that results in a "classy" finish may enable that careless spouse to learn the healthy pride that will motivate better quality.

3. *Above all, avoid words that offend or put the other person down.* You may have to explain that red bandannas that turn elegant, white sheets a shocking pink in the laundry just won't do it. Gently, lovingly correct, *and* supply a suggestion for a better outcome. Always affirm the effort, and appreciate the love that prompts it!

Sharing work has yet another hazard. In most couples one person is a born-and-trained procrastinator. When one gets things done well, promptly, and efficiently, and the other does them only in due time (whatever that is), sparks are inevitable. The slower spouse has good intentions but doesn't see timing as crucial. The efficient one rarely agrees with that view—timing is everything!

Before either fully realizes it, the latter spouse is nagging the former. The more "she" nags, predictably, the more "he" resists. A vicious cycle emerges, which neither can seem to stop.

In your planning time, therefore, I urge you both to stipulate some reasonable time frame. I, personally, have found that asking my husband when he will do a certain task works—*most* of the time. If I tell him I want it done by dinnertime, he feels that I am controlling and "bossy." Under such circumstances he is likely to resist doing it forever.

One bride told me she could get her husband to do almost any job if she collected the tools and equipment and stood by to assist him. These examples sound like procrastination is singularly a male problem, but, of course, it isn't.

As in other problem areas, remaining loving and patient but also clear and definite about your frustration will help.

Who Decides?

Lillian came to my office with her eyes filled with unshed tears. She and Marvin had been married 25 years, and she could not recall his ever suggesting activities they could share. Well, that wasn't quite true. He could find an endless list of jobs to share—painting, gardening, meticulously ordering his shop equipment. He was even willing to help Lillian with grocery shopping and housekeeping tasks.

The problem was, Lillian felt, that Marvin just didn't know how to have fun. She had grown weary of planning their occasional evening out. It began to seem that she was imposing her wishes on a reluctant spouse. She was feeling alternately used and rejected. No wonder the tears were flowing!

This couple were far from being newlyweds, but their 25 years of heartaches could have been prevented. We learned that Marvin had been trained by his hardworking parents that it was wrong to have fun until all the work was done. We all know, of course, that *never* is *all* the work done. Try as we may, there will always be more projects to tackle and tasks to be completed.

To have a sound marriage, there must be a balance in work and play. Some recreational times need to be written into the weekly calendar. And each spouse must be responsible for suggesting and planning that time. If one of you has dictated your activities too much, back off. Suggest some interesting event, but get ideas and wishes from the other as well. Be careful to avoid criticizing the "chooser" if the event turned out badly.

Usually the imbalance is not due to one partner wanting to be the controller. Couples slide, gradually, into such habits. But do work to get out of this routine. Here are some specific suggestions:

1. Take turns being responsible for your fun night.

2. Watch your newspaper and listen to your local radio for upcoming events of value.

3. Create a list of fun activities each of you enjoys, and choose a different one each week.

4. Develop friendships with creative couples who know how to have fun activities.

5. Consider your budget of time as well as money, and plan for events that will not cost too much of either.

6. When your spouse finally takes the risk of planning a date, be sure to express appreciation and don't criticize the choice. There's no more certain way to stop his or her changing than to be bored or critical.

What Is Fun Anyway?

A few years ago a popular bumper sticker asked, "Are we having fun yet?" In the affluence of the past five decades (with a few notable recessions subtracted), pleasure seeking has become a primary goal of many people. There are so many exciting experiences from which to choose that people have become saturated. What *is* fun anyway? Here are a few ideas. Some of them are very costly, but most are easily affordable.

1. Make some special candy or cookies together. I have hilarious and sticky memories of a family taffy pull. Making, filling, and enjoying cream puffs is a delectable experience.

2. Walk to your local ice cream or yogurt shop and enjoy a new flavor. The walk, of course, needs to be long enough to burn up the extra calories.

3. Go to some antique stores and discover the pieces that were like those your grandparents had. You don't *have* to buy them.

4. Visit a shopping area or mall just to test your willpower. Can you have fun wishing together without spending a penny?

5. Take a drive to anyplace nearby that you would visit if you were on vacation. There are a number of such places in my city I've never visited.

6. In nice weather, pack a simple picnic and hike or

drive to a place where you can soak up the sensory richness of nature. Within easy driving distance of most communities are nature preserves, state parks, lakes, and winding country roads. Explore them.

7. Save up for this one. It's expensive but so exotic you'll never forget it: take a hot-air balloon ride! This incomparable experience is not for the fainthearted nor anyone with a fear of heights. But it is a truly unique and indescribably lovely thing to do.

8. Invite special friends over to play Scrabble, Monopoly, or whatever other games you may like. Simple refreshments of popcorn and soda make such an evening fun and easy.

9. Plan next year's vacation. A big part of the fun of vacations lies in the anticipation. By planning well in advance, you can do special things at a lower cost. Plane fares, for example, can be cheaper than driving when you catch the specials.

10. Get up early and watch a sunrise. Not being a morning person, I've done this only a few times in my life, but once my eyes were open, it was a thrill I won't forget.

11. Once in a while, read the same book and discuss it. I'll admit this is risky, but if you can keep it "cool" you'll find it wonderfully stimulating.

12. Share lots of teasing, touching, and laughing together. It takes a lot of self-discipline to let go of the daily little frictions and hurts one unwittingly inflicts on the other, but when you practice the art of loving, the payoff is a glorious marriage. Explore total intimacy of mind, emotions, body, and spirit.

These are only a few of an endless list of fun and rewarding activities you may share. Add many of your own, and you will find you are never bored. Your lives will be beautifully personal and yet harmoniously interwoven.

Sharing Each Other's Interests

Some years ago my husband was an incorrigible numismatist. That word, I so laboriously learned, is the title of the true coin collectors. We were both in school when he became so enamored of this hobby that we cashed the check for our groceries in nickels and dimes so he could pour over each precious piece, seeking that rare, valuable one. It was my choice, then, either to return the coins to the bank for bills or to spend what looked like a Sunday School collection at the store!

Needless to say, I became intensely resentful of his preoccupation with this hobby. Being a determined man (I then called him "stubborn"), however, he would not even consider giving up this interest. In fact, it became increasingly important to him.

In desperation I learned the truth of the old adage "If you can't beat 'em, join 'em!" So I began to attend conventions and auctions with him. On occasion he would display some of his most precious pieces, and I learned how to fold the right shades of velvet fabric to best accent the lovely coins. I met many enjoyable people and developed some lasting friendships among them.

There is a fine balance to be established in allowing husband and wife some private time and interests, yet sharing these in some degree. Such separateness is healthy and can be tolerated only if there is great security in each other's love. If you doubt your commitment, it is very difficult to prove your love. Any time apart or evidence of being engrossed in a personal activity is likely to be perceived as a threat to your relationship. When such an imbalance is there, you are at risk for becoming possessive. Marriages cannot grow strong or be healthy when they are contaminated with the weeds of mistrust, control, and selfishness.

It is urgent that each of you develop some interests

and activities of your own. This may be a hobby, a volunteer activity that benefits others, or a creative craft. As you share these with each other, they will enrich your individuality as well as your relationship.

It is equally important that you keep the priorities of your relationship in order. Watch for hurt feelings and fears of abandonment. Check your spouse's plans and needs before you pursue your own interests. Let your spouse see that your hobby is not more important than his or her love, and be sure your spouse does not feel you want to possess him or her and control his or her life.

I recommend that each spouse find one hobby that expresses his or her creativity that is uniquely his or hers. Many people have lost touch with their creativity and so argue that God left them out when He passed around such gifts. That is absolutely untrue. A Creator as great as God, who created us in His image, has not let one person be void of creativity.

Think about what interests you; look back on your childhood at what brought joy to you. Pick one thing and explore it—just for fun. If it is fun, develop it. Take a class that might inspire some new hobbies. Don't be afraid to explore. Don't expect perfection, but find the rewards of your own pursuit of creativity.

Working, playing, learning, and growing together are some of the building blocks of a strong marriage. Doing activities alone at times can balance the togetherness with individuality. Communicating clearly and lovingly about these activities will also forge a link in your bond of marriage. Weave your activities neatly into the total tapestry of your shared lives.

Reflection and Action

1. In a previous chapter you reflected on shared interests. Identify those things you and your spouse enjoy doing together that have been a recent source of difficulty instead of pleasure.

2. What strengths/weaknesses do each of you have that would be considered out of the traditional mold for your gender role?

   Alone   *As a Team*

   a.   a.

   b.   b.

   c.   c.

3. Identify areas in which you prefer to *work* singly and areas in which you prefer to *work* as a team.

4. If you are a born procrastinator, describe what you experienced as a young person or child, when you put off doing duties or obligations.

   a.

   b.

   c.

5. Identify fun activities that you do *without* your spouse and fun activities you do *with* your spouse. Does the balance seem right?

6. List the appealing / unappealing aspects of your spouse's main interest area(s) and provide your rationale:

   appealing   *unappealing*

6

Communicating Effectively

On and on she rambled, trying to keep calm but wanting desperately to convince Phil that her ideas were right. As I observed Valerie's tense face and clenched fists, I knew her outer calm was a facade. Furthermore, I could guess that Phil's gaze, fixed on the ceiling, meant he was not really hearing her at all.

Phil and Valerie had been talking about money, budgets, vacation plans, and a new car. But their real communication had been about control. If *she* refused to live within the budget he'd worked out, it was just too bad. And if *he* was too stingy to increase that budget, he was simply not a decent husband.

The problem was that this couple were *talking* on one level, *listening*—if at all—on another, but *feeling* on still another level. No wonder they were not communicating!

Effective communication means that both the words and emotions of the speaker are conveyed with reasonable accuracy to the listener. Furthermore, it means the listener and speaker both are responsible to check out that accuracy. Finally, for a communications transaction to be completed, the listener must respond in some meaningful way to the speaker. The acknowledgment of each one's purpose in speaking, validating the meaning, is expressed in a completed transaction.

To communicate successfully demands skills in three basic areas. It takes a great deal of practice to achieve these skills.

1. *Clear thinking.* It is easy to let one's thoughts ramble, to bring up old events, and to jump from one topic to another. Effective communicators do not do this. They stick with the topic at hand, think about it, and distill these thoughts into a few well-chosen words. They are willing to allow the other person to interject comments and do not try to do all the talking. They speak concisely.

Naturally, some conversations are more intense and demand a different kind of input. Casual talk with strangers is much more superficial than an argument with your spouse over a broken budget!

2. *Careful listening.* One of the weakest traits I find in most families with serious problems is the failure to listen attentively. If one does listen, it is often with the hope of finding loopholes in an argument so he or she can win it! The individual may listen to the other person so he or she can find a list of information to store up and use against the person at a later time.

Jeanne was a classic good listener. On their way to a party, her husband was telling a story. Because of its length, it was unfinished when they arrived. After a happy evening, the couple were returning home. "On the way to the party, Honey, you were telling me about your deal at the office today—what happened after the boss started yelling?" Jeanne asked. She remembered his story, reminded him of his stopping point, and cared enough to ask him to finish the narration. It would be easy to stay in love with a wife like Jeanne!

Listening includes two levels. Hearing the words and clarifying their meaning is no small task. It demands thinking and asking questions with an open mind. But active listening has sensitive antennae alert to the emotions that often silently flow beneath the surface. Anxiety commonly is hidden by irritation, and sadness can be masked by a deceptive smile.

3. *Careful reading of body language.* Carol's hazel eyes were weeping copiously. For some strange reason I, usually sensitive and caring, felt irritated. As she wailed out her woes over her "mean" husband, I noticed her hands and the set of her jaw. They were clenched in a manner clearly depicting strong anger. My intuition was more accurate than my eyes. She was trying to make me feel sorry for her when, in fact, she needed to face and deal honestly with her anger.

Learn to look first at your partner's eyes, those "windows of the soul." While they can, like Carol's, deceive you, far more commonly they will reveal the most sensitive, tender feelings from the depths of a soul.

Next look at the mouth and jaws. Are their lips pursed stubbornly, drooping in pain or sadness, or upturned in humor? Perhaps they reveal anger or cynicism. Are the jaws relaxed or tightened with rage? How about the posture? Is the head bowed in grief or erect with defiance? Do the shoulders droop in depression? Are the hands outstretched in an appeal for help? Or are they clenched like Carol's, ready to strike a blow? Perhaps your partner is overwrought with emotions, pacing to and fro.

These are only some of the observations that will reveal truth or deception in your communication with your partner. When feelings are intense, it may be wise to hold back any comment on your observations, because it may seem you are trying to invade your spouse's mind. When he or she becomes calm, however, such observations can nicely clarify transactions between you. They may even help your spouse understand himself or herself more accurately.

When you have mastered the skill of reading the body language of your spouse, practice it on yourself. You may be more aware of physical sensations than visual pictures of yourself. But pay attention to those feelings of tightness in your jaws, shoulders, forehead, or neck. Each of those parts of your body will react to certain emotions. Your forehead may furrow with the lines of worry. Your neck may be saying, "I won't give in," even when it may be best to do so. A stern set of your mouth and jaws may even cause discomfort. Are they telling you that you are the stubborn or unreasonable one this time?

Good communication, you see, includes being sensitive, not only to your partner, but also to yourself. It's up to you to avoid guessing games in interpersonal transactions. When you become aware that you are feeling excited, loving, sad, worried, scared, or angry, stop the conversation briefly. Put your innermost emotions into words, not in an accusing manner, but in order to clarify issues. It will help your partner understand just what issues are at stake. It will help you avoid making decisions based on emotions rather than wisdom. And it almost always will help you avoid those defeating power struggles.

There are at least five levels of communication. Each is appropriate at times, but none is proper all the time.

 1. *The ritual.* An example of a ritual is the ceremony of meeting a stranger. In each culture this ritual varies, but in the Western world we exchange names, shake hands, and make small talk.

Hank never gets beyond rituals with his wife. He has a set routine of describing his day, listening to hers, and then he opens his mail and reads the paper. His rituals rarely vary, and life with him can become boring.

2. *Pastiming.* Waiting in your doctor's office will clearly demonstrate this level of communicating. You will hear people discussing the current "flu" symptoms, the economy, or various political issues. At parties you attend, you will find yourself talking in a superficial manner about topics that really don't matter much. Some couples stick with such unimportant topics that are safe and rarely result in disagreements. While they seem to be really communicating, they fail to realize that they are missing the level of feeling exchange that makes intimacy possible.

3. *Sharing activities.* You've already read the chapter on activity sharing. Here I only want to reiterate the importance of this focus as a new step toward intimacy. In his wonderful book *Four Loves* (San Diego: Harcourt Brace Jovanovich, 1960), C. S. Lewis describes intimacy. It includes the Greek concepts of the agape love of parents and God for children, the phileo love of siblings, and the erotic love of husband and wife. Then he explains an additional love, that of friends. He calls it the "Oh! You too?" love of discovering mutual interest and unfolding fondness, the cherishing of friend by friend. If marriages could be built on these four loves, the divorce courts could close!

4. *Game playing.* In order to gain attention, people play games, writes Eric Berne in *What Do You Say After Hello?* (New York: Bantam Books, 1973). These are not fun games played for entertainment. They are mind games, enacted unconsciously in order to gain close attention of a deeply emotional sort from another person. Such games begin in early childhood, and they serve the purpose of satisfying the feeling needs of youngsters. The habits, unfortunately, become imbedded in the personality and continue, usually destructively, into adult life.

A common example is that of a spouse who found early in life that the best attention came with illness. Such a person (and I was one of them) finds new aches and pains whenever his or her need for nurturing and closeness is not being met. The pain may be physical or emotional, but it is profound and pushes the complainer inexorably. The sufferer searches for a sympathetic listener and will wear that listener out with details of how awful he or she feels, how terribly he or she has been treated, or how hopeless he or she feels. Eventually the sufferer feels relieved and even is grateful to the listener—who is left devastated by the horror of the tales of woe and helpless to heal the pains.

If you or your spouse is creating havoc in your marriage by game playing, stop the habit! Here's how:

 a. *Become aware of what is going on.* The best tipoffs are these: the listener feels terrible while the victim feels relieved; there are no permanent solutions, so the victim returns again and again with unsolvable problems. When answers are proposed, the victim responds, "Yes, but . . ."

 b. *Explain gently but clearly what you perceive.* Help your spouse understand that he or she seems to fail to get better and that you are feeling defeated in attempts to help.

 c. *Silently work at giving all the positive feedback and attention possible.* Stay loving.

 d. *When it is difficult to **feel** loving, work hard at **understanding**.* It feels almost as good to be understood as to be loved. In fact, it is a part of genuine love.

 e. *Stay clear about whose the problem is and what the problem is.* If you take on a problem that is really your spouse's, you are asking for more trouble, and you will find no solutions. You will fall, instead, into the role of the co-dependent, enabling the real problems to continue.

 f. *Don't allow the stronger spouse to assume the responsibility for problems because he or she can solve them.* If, however, those problems belong to the other, you cannot solve them, and by your very efforts you eliminate the need for that partner to deal honestly with the issues. It is at such a point (dealing with the ultimate need and solutions) that a professional counselor may be invaluable. When, and only when, you've used up all of your insights and the help and prayers of friends and pastor, look up a qualified marital counselor. Together, describe the feelings, interactions, and problems that keep you unhappy and helpless. Follow your counselor's advice when it makes sense and fits in with your beliefs, but remember you have the right to disagree and debate points that confuse you.

Your family doctor or minister often are reliable sources for a referral. I suggest you call the counselor, explain your needs, be sure he or she can respect your faith, and decide whether or not this person sounds right for you. I also warn you that if you need to accept some responsibility for problems, it can be painful. Find the courage to face these challenges relating to *your* need to change. Don't give up at that point of discomfort.

5. *Intimacy.* The Latin root word from which this term is derived is *intimus,* meaning "within." According to the 1964 *Webster's New World Dictionary,* the word means "most private or personal" or "closely acquainted, very familiar."

One of the greatest gifts in this world is that of true intimacy with one's spouse. I am blessed with such a relationship. Through deep struggles with each other's pain, we have reached a point at which we are almost totally open and safe with each other. I used the word almost because we each have a few secrets (and they are *very* few) that we share with no one. We do not agree on all issues, but we respect each other's individuality. We recognize each other's feelings and seek out the needs or joys that prompt them. We weep and laugh together. We would rather be with each other than anyone else in the world. One of my greatest discoveries has been the joy of just being silent together. Intimacy is often too immense for words.

Trusting each other when we are apart is another part of intimacy. I know, as does my husband, that we are committed to one another and that no one can come between us. Neither of us is as happy apart as together, though both of us find fun and fulfillment in our own separate lives.

If you are willing to persevere, work, use help, and take risks, you, too, can master the skills of communication. If you add loyalty and trust, you will learn the indescribable joy and love of intimacy. Intimacy pervades the intellect, the emotions, the spirit, and the body. God has truly created a masterpiece in making His children capable of such an experience.

Reflection and Action

Dr. Ketterman writes about the five levels of communication. Look at the list below and provide the information requested.

1. Identify a ritual in which your spouse engages: _____

_____

   a. Ask your spouse to identify one in which you engage: ____

     _____

   b. Do you agree with your spouse's selection; does your spouse agree with you? _____

2. Give an example of an "Ain't it awful!" conversation you've heard recently _____

_____

3. Give an example of a "Yes, but . . ." conversation:_____

_____

4. Give an example of how the "problem solver" works:

_____

_____

5. Look up the words *intimacy* and *trust* in a dictionary. Select words or terms that expand their meaning and write a brief paragraph:

7

Coping with Personality Differences

It was easy to understand how Ben and Jeanette had been attracted to each other. They were total opposites! Ben was easygoing, laid back, reliable, and responsible. Jeanette enlivened him with her energy, her emotional intensity, and her impulsive ways. He loved her impromptu ideas for a shopping trip or hike and picnic. But Ben would never think of such a fun event on his own.

Over time, however, the traits that had magnetized their lives became the source of great tension and frightening frustration. Some years after their marriage, Jeanette began to feel the inevitable stress of always being the one to think of activities. She could hardly tolerate Ben's methodical, plodding style of setting about a list of household repairs. She began to employ her intense energy to fuss and nag at him.

Calm Ben rarely responded to his wife's fussing, and it never really made sense to him. He was just being who he was, and he had believed she loved him for that. But now he began to feel she was trying to transform him into someone he could never be.

Jeanette, in turn, thought Ben was simply stubborn, unwilling to change or to please her. She became angry and treated Ben unkindly, retaliating for his perceived meanness.

This couple is typical of many. Usually their problems are based on misperceptions and misunderstandings. Years of research have revealed a number of inborn temperamental traits. A cherished friend of mine was part of such a research team many years ago. He told me that one experiment included raising the temperature in a newborn nursery only three degrees. Most of the infants squirmed and fussed for a short time, then adapted and behaved exactly as they had before the change. A few of them showed no reaction at all, and a few others reacted with intense movements and loud crying that lasted for hours.

As these babies became older, they and their families were repeatedly studied. And guess what? The team discovered that those early habits persisted. Those who adjusted to the temperature change tended to adapt pretty well to all the variations life brought them. Those who reacted not at all tended, like Ben, to sail undisturbed through life's challenges, while the heavy reactors fought their way through life, figuratively kicking and screaming all the way.

Most of you are already identifying yourselves and your partners in one of these three categories. Let me try to slow you down. There are many tests that analyze and help you understand your personality and that of your spouse. It may well be worth your time and money to visit a good psychologist and take some of these tests.

One good friend and her husband took a test called the Meyers-Briggs. After it had been interpreted to her, she exclaimed, "No wonder Carl refuses to read the books I give him! He's intuitive—not judgmental." She understood that he relied more on that sixth sense, and to him the logic of reading in order to form good judgments was a waste of time.

The studies I mentioned earlier, however, contain helpful information. You can easily study the facts that follow and evaluate yourself and your spouse. It won't cost you a penny. Here are nine traits present in all personalities to some degree. Most of us fit somewhere in the center, but a fair number of people are on one extreme or the other. When people of two different extremes have to live together, sparks tend to fly!

1. *Activity level.* Jeanette was highly energetic, and it was difficult for her to tolerate Ben's laid-back, easygoing manner. He appeared lazy to her, and she seemed manic to him.

2. *Distractibility.* Ben was born with the ability to stick solidly to whatever he was doing until he was done with it. Jeanette, by contrast, often left one task for two others, finishing none of them. Ben had great difficulty tolerating what he considered flightiness.

3. *Intensity level.* Some people speak loudly, and others seem to whisper. In times of grief one wails desperately, while the other may seem not to care. In Ben's case, grief could overwhelm him, but it was not easy for him to give expression to it unless he was alone. Jeanette would express anger and sadness intensely, but these emotions were short-lived. Neither understood that the other was born this way.

4. *Regularity (predictability).* Ben was so predictable that Jeanette feared becoming bored with him. She was so irregular that Ben became afraid of her flare-ups and was exhausted by her quick ups and downs.

It is apparent that each of these traits has extremes that create problems. When individuals find somewhat of a middle position, they will get along more easily, but those who naturally fall on extremes must work to moderate their traits. Above all, each needs to understand the other's being born with some basic differences that can never be totally changed.

’ 5. *Persistence.* This can be a strong trait that enables one to stick with a task until it is done or a problem until it is solved. On the other hand, it can cause a person to stick with a wish or demand that opposes the partner's ideas. When persistence becomes stubborn selfishness, power struggles develop. Rarely does anyone win in such a case.

’ 6. *Sensory threshold.* This means that people vary in their awareness of and sensitivity to physical stimuli. Light, sound, taste, and touch are examples of stimuli with which we are all familiar. For some of us, just as in the example of the newborn infants, even a thunderclap causes no startle reflex. For others, however, a door's slam or a clock's tick can create a shock or be an annoyance. If your spouse's sensitivities are the opposite of yours, you may have a hard time living with him or her. It may help you to know he or she is not "faking" it but that he or she was just born supersensitive (or apparently numb!).

’ 7. *Withdrawal (from new situations).* Some people never know a stranger. Others struggle even to shake hands with a new employee at work. Neither quality, once again, is good or bad in itself. But if you are gregarious and your spouse is content with only one longtime friend, you are likely to feel frustrated and isolated. You will both need to discuss your desires and negotiate some ways to meet both of your personality demands. The reserved one can learn to act interested in others, and the outgoing one may need to join some groups that do not require the other's presence.

A word of caution is needed here. It is easier than you think to grow apart at such a point. Be very careful to keep your activities balanced. Save plenty of time for each other, avoid judging each other, and work hard at understanding your spouse and yourself. Let me remind you—even though you are born with different traits, you can modify them to some extent. But do not blame one another for being the way you were born.

8. *Adaptability*. Changes are constant in life. From temperature to health and from finances to feelings, change is certain. Some of us can flow with those changes easily, while others seem never to adapt. Trying to understand and cope with a mate from an opposite extreme is not easy. It can, in fact, sap much of one's energy, leaving little for just loving and enjoying each other. But with insight and patience, each can learn to understand and support the other in moving toward a better balance.

9. *Mood*. We have come to see this word as a negative term. Someone who is moody is usually considered to be grouchy. But actually one may know a range of moods from elation to calmness, from anxiety to anger. Once again, research showed that some babies seem happy and bouncy from the early weeks of life. Others are born with a scowl that gets only more fixed with time. The frowners seem to be irritated with the chronically happy people. The chronically happy, in turn, cannot comprehend why the negative-mood people seem unable to get happy.

Let me explain that there is an almost infinite variety of combinations of these traits. That is, one may be highly sensitive to neurological stimulation of all kinds but respond in a mild degree. Another may have a high energy and activity level but is highly focused and persistent.

It is indeed a challenge to understand a spouse who is highly variable. But the more you step back emotionally and observe, the more clearly you will decipher the pattern. It is of crucial importance that you understand these qualities and the major differences between you in each of them. Look for the best ways you can work at modifying your most intense traits. If it irritates you when your partner is not predictable, and you by nature need predictability, see if he or she will, for example, post a schedule on your calendar one day at a time.

I recommend that every couple reserve from 5 to 15 minutes every evening to talk specifically about needs and schedules. When one of you has a hard day, the other can help a bit more and be comforting and encouraging. No matter what your personality traits may be, you can try to understand your mate and reach out to meet those special needs during tough times.

One huge error most couples make is to suppose their spouses can anticipate their needs and read their minds. Many *parents* can do that, so it is easy to expect one's spouse to do likewise. Because he or she grew up in an environment that is different from yours, that expectation will greatly mislead you—so be sure that each of you spells out clearly on a regular basis how you feel and what it is that you need.

It may be difficult at times for you to define just what you need. Some of you, like me, have tried hard all your lives to be totally self-reliant. You have ignored your feelings and denied those needs. As stress builds within any marriage, however, your resources and self-strengths will not always be adequate. It's OK to need! In fact, sharing deep feelings and their attendant needs will bond you together in a more truly loving unity than if you were too independent. Just be careful not to take advantage of your partner's needs and use them to belittle or manipulate.

Perhaps you can use some guidelines to help you adjust to a spouse whose personality is very different from yours.

1. *Avoid judging.* The Bible is intensely clear in its command to avoid judging. It is easier than you would think to believe that those who see things differently from you are automatically wrong. When you read this, you can see such an attitude is downright arrogant. Opposites

classically attract, and this enlivens a relationship. Enjoy each other's differences.

2. *React slowly.* No matter how intense you are, make yourself stop and think before you react to that particularly annoying trait of your spouse. You love it when he or she returns the favor to you.

3. *Remember: understanding and forgiving do not mean condoning.* If your spouse, highly intent and persistent, harangues and verbally abuses you, that's unacceptable behavior. So you can be prepared to say something like this: "Sweetheart, I know your feelings are strong and it's hard for you to let go of an issue. But I also know you love me and wouldn't want to hurt me. The way you just laid into me for failing to have dinner ready on time really hurt my feelings. I explained that I had to work late. Let's both take some time out and talk this out later. I don't want to go to bed hurt and angry."

4. *Remember: forgiving does heal old hurts.* Once you understand your spouse and yourself, forgiving becomes possible. Entire books on forgiving are available. Know that the forgiver is blessed even more than the offender. By admitting the hurts, finding out why the abusive person said or did such a painful thing, and then allowing those facts to penetrate the heart, creating profound understanding, you can forgive permanently.

Such forgiving is better when it is accompanied by a plan to prevent the hurt from being perpetrated again. That plan may include the following steps:

1. *Provide information about how he or she hurt you.* This step needs to include your specific area of vulnerability, as well as the hurtful action of the offender.

2. *Strike a mutual agreement to avoid situations that could repeat such an offense.* By this, I mean that a battle for control can be prevented by learning to negotiate or take turns.

3. *Work on building self-esteem and mutual respect,* which are basic in the prevention of battles with their many wounds.

4. *With all the control you can muster, avoid criticizing each other to outsiders.* The more you discuss each other's faults, the more magnified they become. Stick with helping each other make the needed changes in behaviors.

5. *When such changes are impossible to effect by yourselves, seek counsel.* Professionals can administer a number of tests to help you understand your personalities and how they impact behaviors. You really cannot change an inborn personality, but marriage counseling can enable each of you to modify how you think and act.

6. *Be precise.* Set small goals for change that are possible to reach.

7. *Follow through.* The best plans in the world are of no use unless you work them. Personality differences may be described in many terms. There are various paper-and-pencil tests that describe and evaluate them. The differences may cause frustration and separation if you interpret actions wrongly. Or they can enrich your marriage and bring about a healthy balance if you understand and use them properly.

If you are in a marriage that seems to be failing or is causing pain, consider the possibility of a serious personality conflict. On your own you may analyze just what these variations are and even make the needed adjustments. If you can't do this alone, seek good professional help. Find someone who truly believes in marriage and will work with you to create a healthy one.

The work required for personality adjustments is immense—but the joy that results makes all the effort worthwhile.

Reflection and Action

1. Draw nine sets of parallel lines representing you and your spouse. Label each set according to the nine personality traits discussed by Ketterman. Label your lines like this example:

Low————————High
Low————————High
Activity Level

Chart your location, as well as that of your spouse, on each of the nine continuums.

2. After you chart your position, have your spouse chart your location. Compare each chart. What were the similarities? differences? How accurate is each chart? If there are disparities, does this indicate a need for further sharing and clarification regarding this particular personality trait?

3. Identify the most important areas of adjustment where there is disparity between your location on the continuum and that of the one made by your spouse.

8

Dependence Versus Independence

So many of the patterns from which marriages are formed originate in childhood. The habits that emerge from those early experiences become automatic. We react and feel in certain circumstances precisely as we did early on. The problem is, of course, that one's spouse always comes ready-made from a different set of situations with varying templates for building a family.

Marie and Len are examples of how this dynamic works. Marie grew up with parents who made most of the family's decisions. She trusted their good judgment and protective love, so it was natural for her to comply with their management. In choosing her husband, Marie looked for a man who was strongly decisive. In Len she found that person. Confident and capable, he was quite at home taking charge.

In the few areas where Marie's expertise was greater than his, however, Len sometimes forgot to allow her the decision-making prerogative. She had to remind him that in menu planning, decorating, and running the household, she needed to make the choices most of the time. Together they negotiated and harmonized the power it took to create a smoothly functioning family.

In this case, the more dependent wife was blessed to

find an independent husband. And yet he was confident enough to allow her to take control where she could comfortably do so. It does, by the way, take an emotionally healthy person to share control with another.

David and Renee were quite another example. Both were oldest children and very responsible. Beyond responsibility, though, each was by temperament fiercely independent. To add to their predicament, both were somewhat insecure. When one tried to make a decision, the other feared being dominated and would automatically oppose that. You can well imagine the regularity and intensity of their battles.

These two eventually required marriage counseling to establish some balances in their battle for control. Such couples will usually need professional help at some point; otherwise, there will be one of three results: one will be broken in spirit and become like a slave to the other, each will continue to fight for control in a miserable marriage, or a divorce will end the struggles.

Another scenario is that of Denise and Mike. Each of these persons was considerate, kind, and dependent. The appearance of the perfect spouse, always deferring to the other, seemed idyllic. As time wore on, however, decisions that needed to be made became mountainous. Responsibilities were seldom completed, and both became anxious and unhappy.

Both Mike and Denise had difficulty making decisions. Each required a good deal of caretaking and felt neglected when that was lacking. Sometimes they both suffered feelings of neglect and frustration, though one or the other could occasionally rally enough strength to cope with crises that inevitably occurred. Their marriage was dangerously weakened by excessive dependency in both of them.

Creation of Dependency

There are several stages through which each personality must grow to become mature. Let's briefly review them:

1. *Trust.* From birth to two years of age, the very foundation of a healthy personality is formed. The unconditional acceptance of a child with his or her inborn traits is crucial. This parental love will respond consistently to a baby's needs with strength and comfort. Parents will show their pride in the child's development and encourage the intimacy that results in good bonding.

In the course of early child care, it is easy for parents to overprotect, make too many of the child's choices, and keep him or her too close. Toward the end of this period, children need to be allowed to explore some (with careful observation). They need to begin to become a bit more free of the parents' care.

2. *Autonomy (childhood independence).* From two to three years, more or less, children fairly abruptly hop off their parents' laps and struggle mightily to have their own way. Every good parent knows that two-year-olds are not ready to take care of themselves or make all their own decisions.

They know equally well that this is the time to teach them good choices. So they let them pick one of two outfits to wear or one of two cereals to eat for breakfast. Good parents set clear, firm boundaries but encourage plenty of exploring and activities within those limits.

Once again, you can see that parents whose boundaries are too tight or too flexible can create dependency in a child. Punishing too harshly for testing the limits is likely to create a fearful, dependent child, or an angry, rebellious one.

3. *Initiative.* From three to five years of age, children's main task is to develop a sense of doing things creatively on their own. Some kids are more capable than others and

will start, with blocks or toys, complex projects that take a good deal of time and energy. When parents praise and facilitate such activities, the child is likely to become confident and will dare more independent functioning.

When parents are overly involved, however, the child may learn to lean on them. Such dependency can easily become a habit that lasts on into adult life. This is especially likely when the child is born with a more laid-back, overly compliant set of traits.

4. *Responsibility.* The elementary school years (ages 5 to 12) are the era of learning a sense of duty. There are some things in life for which the child alone is responsible—for example, studying, getting along with peers and teachers, keeping some order in life, and helping out in family work projects.

Once again we see the impact of wise parenting in furthering healthy independence. Good parenting skills in this time frame include the assignment of jobs around the home. Such skills require teaching, because kids do not automatically know how to accomplish many of these assignments. Learning how to organize, attack, and complete these mechanical tasks, however, teaches children the skills that will enable them to succeed in even greater complexities of school life.

Parents who require too little of their children create a carefree attitude that is part of excessive dependency. Requiring too much, on the other hand, helps form an adult who feels it necessary to take on every responsibility, allowing the spouse to lean too much. You can see how vital the proper balances in life really are.

5. *Independence.* It is in the teen years that adult independence is established. As you know, that is a gradual process that requires years of time. Whether or not parents allow it, teenagers make many of their own decisions. For better or worse, teens choose their friends, their style

of dressing, and their study habits. In families where wise decision-making is taught, teens become capable of healthy independence.

Without adequate guidance, however, teens often make poor decisions or none, drifting along through life with neither goals nor an anchor. When such young people approach marriage, they are ill-equipped in the area of reasonable independence. If two drifters marry, you can see why a successful relationship may be hard to accomplish. If you are in this enlarging group, you will need to work hard to think your way into a reasonable degree of independence.

Parents who are too strict and make too many decisions for their teenagers also create problems for them. By making too many choices, parents deprive teens of the experience that is one of their best teachers. Teens in these families usually either rebel or become too dependent.

It is the proper balance in any life situation that is crucial to happy, successful living. As you look back over your life, you may see how your parents taught you. Did they overprotect you? Were they too strict, making too many decisions for you? Or did they give you too much freedom and too little guidance?

When you understand the strengths and weaknesses in your developing years, you will be better able to make the needed adjustments in your dependence-independence balances. Here are those suggestions about how to evaluate yourself and make any needed changes in the degree of your independence.

~ 1. *Are you able to manage your time, money, and energy reasonably well?* If so, you will not run up high balances on your credit cards. You will usually accomplish the necessary basic tasks every day. You will have enough energy left to play with your spouse and enjoy fun activities.

~ 2. *Are you able to make most of your decisions success-*

fully? You can know this is so if your decisions do not hurt others and if their outcomes are good for you.

3. *Do you labor over decisions or second-guess yourself?* By this I mean, for example, that you can make a purchase with only a reasonable amount of comparing and deliberating. After the purchase, you enjoy the item and do not agonize over the "what ifs" or "if onlys" that may torment you.

4. *Do you always have to make the final decision?* People who are too independent have difficulty negotiating or taking turns.

5. *Are you unduly in need of others' approval, or do you know when you do a job well?*

6. *Are you too indifferent to the opinions of others?* People with healthy independence can give themselves a pat on the back, but they also are sensitive to the feelings and opinions of others. They do not want to offend or hurt another person.

7. *How well do you tolerate being alone?* Independent people enjoy time alone and are capable of filling time with a good balance of rest and creative, enjoyable activities.

8. *Do you, on the other hand, hibernate, avoiding others?* Such seclusiveness may indicate excessive independence or the extreme shyness that is often a part of too much dependency.

You can see that there are no good or bad answers to these questions. It is either extreme to which you may go that means you may have trouble in your marriage.

If you are extremely dependent or independent, chances are your marriage will suffer. Once in a while, like Marie and Len, a strongly independent spouse will enjoy a dependent partner. My experience reveals that in time, however, even strong people feel exhausted by too much dependency.

Without realizing it, a more independent spouse may encourage the partner's dependency. A couple I once knew demonstrate this principle. The wife, whom I'll call Debra, realized early in her marriage that her husband, Nick, was too dependent. He delayed decisions and abdicated responsibilities. More and more reluctantly, Debra assumed Nick's duties. She assumed the bookkeeping first. Later she repaired broken items around the house or called expensive repairmen to do so.

Nick lost job after job, and eventually Debra found herself supporting Nick financially. She tried to encourage him and build up his faltering ego, but with little success. Had she refused to assume Nick's responsibilities early on, he might have learned out of necessity to carry his share of the load. The story still may not have ended perfectly, but chances are Debra would not have ended up far overburdened and very short of respect for her spouse.

What can you do to change your own imbalance in dependency and also reverse negative trends in your marriage?

1. *Make a commitment to change.* Review your habits and feelings. Ask your spouse and a friend or relative. If all these sources of information concur, chances are that you need to decide to bring about a change.

2. *Make a plan.* No change simply happens. You must take the action. Such a plan needs to include such steps as these:

> a. Practice making one or more (or fewer) decisions daily. Do this on your own, and risk the results.
>
> b. Learn to think through debatable or brand-new ideas and risk discussing them. If you are too independent, learn to defer to others.
>
> c. Be prepared to suffer the consequences of any mistakes you make, and learn from them. Do not give up and quit.

d. Gradually give up taking charge too much, and share decision-making with your partner.

e. Kindly refuse to accept a dependent spouse's "dumping" of responsibilities on you, or discipline yourself to stop doing the dumping.

f. Learn to think positively or realistically about yourself. If you feel inadequate, look for your strengths; if you are overly confident, admit your imperfections (few as they may be!).

g. Keep a record of your successes in changing so you can measure your progress.

3. *Find a friend to cheer you on.* All change of significance is not only difficult but even frightening. You may experience defeats or brag about unreal progress. An honest, trusted friend can help you stay on track.

4. *Refuse to quit.* You will often be tempted to stop. You'll convince yourself that it's not worth the work, that you'll never make it, or that if you do it won't last. Eliminate negative thoughts by disciplining yourself to think positively.

5. *Rejoice in your ultimate success.* Some changes I worked on took several years from start to automatic finish. You can make it.

Above all, remember that you have a loving and powerful Heavenly Father. He wants you to find balance and wholeness in your life. Seek His help and use it. He certainly will uphold you and see you through. You will be delighted with the healthy balance in your own life and in your marriage.

Reflection and Action

Using the chart below, complete the following exercise:

1. Column 1 indicates the approximate age level. In column 2 next to each level, list the critical issue or character element that is worked on during this stage.

2. In column 3, write your personal appraisal of the level you have achieved with words like *strong, adequate, good, fair, need improvement, potential problem area,* etc.

3. Write out an action plan for dealing with each area you have identified as "needing improvement." Use the five strategies listed by Ketterman in your text.

Column 1	Column 2	Column 3
Teens		
5-12		
3-5		
2-3		
0-2		

9

Developing Personal Character

To build a healthy marriage and create a sound family demands good *character,* a word not used much in today's culture. Yet the time-honored Webster's dictionary defines *character* in depth. The word comes from a Greek term meaning "to engrave." One definition relates to the distinctive mark of an object or person—the distinctive trait, quality, or attribute thereof. Character is also an individual's unique pattern of personality or behavior. It may mean one's moral constitution, strength, self-discipline, or fortitude. One's character determines one's reputation.

Historically, character is described through the presence in an individual of the four cardinal virtues:

1. *Prudence.* Prudence is the capability of exercising sound judgment in practical, daily matters. It is the quality cluster of caution, discretion, sensibility, and circumspection. I know too few marriages in which these qualities are consistently present.

2. *Justice.* This quality implies righteousness, impartiality, and fairness. Marital discord would be rare indeed if both spouses practiced this virtue.

3. *Temperance.* The root words for this term mean that there is a proper mix of qualities. Tempered steel, for example, contains exactly the right amounts of iron, carbon, nickel, and chromium. It is formed under precise amounts of heat and pressure to create the needed hardness and flexibility. The tempering of character also demands the special ingredients of morality, integrity, love, patience, goodness, humility, and honor. It takes the heat of tribulations and the pressure of life's challenges to produce the character trait of temperance.

4. *Fortitude.* This quality is one of quiet strength. It is the ability to endure great adversity patiently. One husband I know lives with a wife who has endured severe pain for more than 20 years. She has developed fortitude through learning to live with pain, and he through finding ways to cherish and encourage her in her pain-filled life.

Another husband I know demonstrates fortitude in a more unusual way. No matter how he tried, Delbert could not please Erin, his wife. She criticized his speech, his manner of dress, his extended family, and his attempts to help her. For years he gently tried to defend himself, to help her find some good thing in him, to feel she loved and respected him. Nothing changed Erin's critical, harsh spirit.

But softly in Del's spirit there grew a sense of fortitude. He could rise above her nagging and find his worth in the value he knew God had placed on him. He accepted the heat and pressure of her criticism and grew more in temperance. To avoid her extreme unfairness, he became more fair and impartial—justice was one of his virtues. And to avoid retaliating by criticizing Erin to others, he exercised that wonderful virtue of prudence.

Instead of continued bickering and outright fights, he learned to transcend the pain. Through his faith and right thinking, Delbert sailed through a tumultuous marriage with unerring strength of character. He could certainly have justified a divorce in many people's eyes. It would have been easier and may have been a relief too. But that course would have prevented the strengthening and deepening of his character.

To build a healthy marriage requires the strong character that rests on those cardinal virtues. To maintain a happy marriage demands a sense of humor and a constant commitment to forgiving one another. To make a lasting marriage requires patience and the ability to look beyond the present. Having the will to look down the road past this day will provide a perspective that will see you through the most difficult days.

How can you build a strong character? Let's take each of those cardinal virtues and think about its development.

1. *Prudence.* This is the exercise of sound judgment in the everyday matters of life. Certainly this quality is closely akin to wisdom—the ability to apply facts or knowledge to daily problems.

Perhaps you grew up without being taught how to make sound judgments or smart decisions. Here are the steps to learning these skills.

> a. *Gather facts.* In any situation such as a disagreement or a required decision, take time to ferret out information. The more facts you can glean, the more satisfactory your solutions will be. Facts are found through asking, listening, reading, and thinking. It takes time to do this research, and some issues are small enough that you need to do only a little patient considering. If you are buying a car or a house, however, you will want to take plenty of time and do your exploring thoroughly. Avoid becoming obsessive and procrastinating decision-making too long.

> b. *List your possible options.* These may include, for example, "Do it now," "Don't do it at all," or "Do it later." With the facts you have collected,

chances are you can come up with a good choice out of the possibilities.

   c. *Make the decision or choice.* This will be frightening for those of you who are not so independent. But make up your mind firmly, and take the plunge. Very likely you will survive to make another prudent decision.

   d. *Sit back and await the consequences.* Positive results will reinforce your confidence. Even negative results, however, are OK if you learn from them. In fact, some of the greatest lessons I've learned have been the result of mistakes I've made.

   e. *Stick with the plan.* When things don't turn out as you would like, it's tempting to give up the process you are trying. But being consistent and tenacious will usually enable you to win.

2. *Justice.* Remember its definition? It means righteousness, impartiality, and fairness. Cultivating these qualities demands immense willpower and, at times, self-sacrifice, but the rewards are great.

   a. In all considerations, focus on what is right or best for those involved. It is a common habit to seek one's own way, trying to prove one is right. Instead, think consistently about the most beneficial outcome for everyone involved.

   b. Learn to think objectively. You may know that you are partial to the color blue or to brown-eyed kids. But perhaps blue does not work in the decorating scheme. And maybe you will not have a brown-eyed child. Can you give up your personal wishes in order to achieve impartiality?

   c. Even more pertinent is the possibility that you would make excuses for the wrongdoing of a person you like. If someone you hold in disfavor did the same thing, would you equally excuse him or her? Justice demands that sort of fairness.

3. *Temperance.* For most of my life I believed temperance was the refusal to drink alcoholic beverages. Then I learned that it meant a sense of moderation in all things. Now I have a more comprehensive definition that fits the concept of character formation.

It was during my high school years that I first learned about "tempered" steel. In an assembly program an itinerant lecturer told us about the sword of Damocles. This amazing weapon had been precisely formed so that it was sharp enough to shave a tough beard, strong enough to attack a fierce enemy, but flexible enough to bend into a perfect circle.

It took a precise blend of ingredients and careful methods to manufacture this unique sword. Similarly, a temperate person is formed from a specific blend of materials under pressure. Let me use myself as a example.

a. I endured losses. My joyful place in the family was usurped by the advent of a beautiful baby sister. My health and even my life were threatened by a series of illnesses. Family members died. Through the losses, my character was being tempered.

b. I suffered deprivation. During the dark years of the dust bowl, our farm crops were lost. In the agonizing years of the Great Depression, our family of 10 went without many things, wore hand-me-down or secondhand clothes, and had no money for some periods of time. The deprivation became an ingredient giving me endurance and a tough sort of strength.

c. I lived through a terrible war. All my courage and faith were essential to surviving the drafting of my friends and my brother into the armed forces. All of us wondered how God could allow the atrocities of war to wound our world so deeply. The trying of our faith worked patience as we saw our world struggle to rebuild.

     d. I endured tight rules and strict discipline. How often I chafed under the unbending boundaries established by my protective parents! Yet that endurance helped me through the many years of nearly intolerable demands of medical and post-medical school training.

Obviously you cannot relive my life, nor would I wish my vicissitudes on you. But you can review your own trials and hurts. Many people bemoan their tough times and become embittered over mistreatment, real or imagined. Instead, you can allow even the memory of those events to strengthen and mellow your character. Knowing you survived abuse of deprivation can assure you that you will make it through other difficulties that may assail you.

So make a list of all the painful events of your life. After recalling the anguish, discipline your mind to dig out the useful lessons you mastered. Think about the fibers of real strength each of these times wove into your character. Thank God for trusting you not only to survive but to use these heartaches to help others.

You may not have been aware of it, but in retrospect I suspect you will see God's hand guiding and protecting you through your difficulties. I do not believe God sends all tough times to us. But I know He sees us through them or redeems us out of them.

    4. *Fortitude.* Slang expressions come and go, but one that is meaningful to me is "guts." In speaking of one who shows unusual courage, we used to say, "He's got guts!" In an attempt to refine this crude word, we ultimately revised the statement like this: "He's got intestinal fortitude!" Whatever term you choose, fortitude is the dignified core of the last of the cardinal virtues. And here are some ideas to help you cultivate it.

     a. *"Be strong in the Lord, and in the power of his might"* (Eph. 6:10). At a time when I felt particularly powerless, I stumbled on the practical validity of this command of Paul. A fine floor lamp in my office was not lighted, and the room was dark. I turned the switch and checked the bulb and discovered that they worked, but still there was no light. At last I traced the cord and discovered it was disconnected from the power source. Simply plugging it in created the miracle of light.

Trying to be strong in ourselves reminds me of that lamp. God's power is there for us, just as the electrical power was waiting in my wall. We simply forget that it takes an act of our will to insert the plugs of our lives into that power source. He rarely jumps out at us but patiently awaits our awakening and choosing to give ourselves as conduits through which His love can flow.

b. *Accept the challenges and hurdles in our paths.* It would be much easier for a track runner to run around the hurdles instead of jumping over them. But anyone who did so would promptly be disqualified. Taking the easy way out of interpersonal struggles by sarcastically saying, "Whatever!" is tempting. But choosing to think objectively, putting aside your selfish desire to get your own way or to pout—and sticking with the issue—can harmoniously settle it.

c. *Practice the almost-lost art of self-control.* The person who can control his or her own tongue and rule his or her own spirit can master almost any situation. A dear friend of mine, Emily, recently discovered that her temper fits were destroying her marriage. She decided to trade in the false power of rage for the true strength of explicit information. She tells her husband now that he has hurt her feelings and explains kindly what will enable that pain to be erased.

d. *Learn to walk away from battles no one can win.*

No matter how good a person your spouse is, he or she will at times be unreasonable. If and when you reach such an impasse, kindly and firmly withdraw. Explain that both of you are too emotional or too self-focused and that you will talk about or decide the matter later. Few issues have to be decided immediately. Taking time out in a friendly (not a pouting) manner will prevent most family feuds.

e. *Practice courage.* A great many people define courage as being unafraid. Actually, such a view is brashness or downright ignorance. When there is danger, all reasonable people experience fear. Such fear may be life-saving. Courage is the determination to face a grave danger when necessary, no matter how frightened one is, in order to protect oneself or a loved one.

f. *Constantly focus not on the easiest but the best solutions to life's dilemmas.* Then discipline yourself to work out those solutions.

There are other qualities that embellish character. Some that you may consider are nobility, honor, benevolence, purity, sanctity, morality, and integrity. It would require a dictionary to name and explain them all. You may choose one or several to perfect in your own life.

The few we've considered can serve as a pattern for you. Read about each one—think and pray about them. Choose one, and then work hard to practice it as well as you can.

What a marriage you can have when each of you perfects the best character possible with the help of God!

Reflection and Action

PRUDENCE	JUSTICE
TEMPERANCE	FORTITUDE

1. Write your own definition of each of the four cardinal virtues listed above:

    a.

    b.

    c.

    d.

2. Identify any area or issue in your life that you believe would benefit from adopting a prudence-based approach: _____

    _____

3. List one area in your life in which you displayed an adequate sense of justice: _____

4. Identify the top three most painful events in your life. Review the four cardinal virtues. Did you apply them to these situations? What was the result?

   a.

   b.

   c.

10

Sound Commitment

"I've filed for divorce!" said the voice on the other end of my telephone line. "I think I've fallen out of love with her. She's sloppy and overweight. I shouldn't have to put up with her crying and nagging all the time!"

The harsh words made no allusion to any faults on his side of the marriage, and he deflected my suggestion that we take a look at the entire scene before he slipped away forever. He seemed not to mind leaving his five-year-old son. His happiness was the only important consideration.

Even more disquieting is the story of Neal and Trish. They had been married less than two years when they divorced. The only explanation Neal could find was "I guess our marriage just ran its course."

Real commitment to a spouse is becoming increasingly rare in our Western society. Divorce rates are at 50 percent of the marriage rate and climbing. Loose, uncommitted relationships are all too common, and security in each other's love may be hard to find.

Many well-conducted studies indicate that healthy marriages and families are built on six pillars of strength:

1. Commitment to each other and the family unit.
2. The capacity to cope with crises constructively.

3. Clear communication that is open and honest.

4. An affirming, appreciative attitude.

5. Regular sharing of activities, both work and play.

6. The practice at home of the family's religious beliefs and traditions.

Throughout this book, you have read about most of these pillar-principles. Now we will think together about commitment.

Threats to Commitment

There are five specific threats to commitment we will consider in this chapter. Undoubtedly you will think of others, but these should enable you to be aware of the existence of all threats and to prevent their breaking up your marriage.

Crises and Losses

Lori returned home from work one Saturday evening to find a couple of acquaintances in her living room with her husband. It had been a long week, and she had looked forward to a quiet evening alone with Paul.

The angry, anxious expressions on the faces she saw, however, did not suggest a fun evening out. The facts spilled out quickly and with shocking, searing pain. The husband of the visiting couple was accusing her beloved Paul of having an affair with his wife, a secretary with whom Paul worked.

Lori at first believed it was only a jealous husband's fears. Paul would never betray his commitment to her! As the other wife acknowledged the truth of these accusations, Lori's trust began to crumble. And when she saw the guilt and anxiety on Paul's face, she knew it was true.

Somehow both of these marriages survived. Paul repented, and Lori found the grace to forgive. The affair left its scars of doubt and pain, but scar tissue is tough once it heals. And Lori and Paul's marriage eventually was stronger for having endured the pain of this affair and survived its blows.

One of the most painful and common crises in marriages is the occurrence of an affair. Studies vary on the extent to which unfaithfulness happens, but clearly a solid majority of married men admit to affairs and close to half of the wives do too.

One report indicates that 55 percent of these affairs, just like Paul's, begin with someone at work. As moral values decline and the character of people across the board is weakened, it is predictable this tragic crisis will increase. When affairs happen repeatedly and when children's values are violated by knowing of a parent's wrongdoing, it may be necessary to consider separation or divorce. I believe this is a last resort and should be considered only when counseling, prayer, and hard work have failed to restore or create a healthy marriage.

Other crises that may crash upon any marriage include illness or injury, job loss, natural disasters, and other huge upheavals. Only today I learned of a family in such a crisis predicament. The wife had lost her job of some 20 years. Her husband had suffered a crippling injury that prevented his working, and they had no insurance. Such stories have been all too familiar in our uncertain economic times.

Bad as they are, however, it is not these cataclysmic events that most afflict marriages. It is, instead, the little catastrophes that occur daily that erode the solid foundations you may have built.

One husband actually threatened to leave his wife because she failed to keep his shirt buttons sewed on. He did not know that men can learn to sew on buttons as well as women, nor did he consider the fact that she had countless tasks to accomplish in making a home for him and their five children. She, on the other hand, had stumbled onto a way she could get even with her husband for failing to meet her expectations. It took considerable work for this couple to stop fighting, communicate honestly, and renew their commitment to each other.

Whatever your crisis, you can use it as Lori and Paul did to build an even stronger, more realistic marriage. Another balance you need is that between idealism and reality. When Lori's husband fell from his pedestal to the clay-footed man he really was, she lost her ideal. By staying with him and working through the hurts, he became to her a real man with strength and weakness whom she could love and help as he in turn helped her.

Boredom

"You're just not fun anymore!" said Barry to his wife, Elise. "We used to have parties and go out with friends. We don't do anything exciting these days." His statements were true, but he had not considered the entire scenario. They now had three children. The demands of the family were draining both of them of their former energy.

Furthermore, he had not dared to mention the fact that a cute young woman at work had been flirting with him outrageously. Any well-worn, loving wife has difficulty competing with a glamorous career girl. With increasing numbers of men staying at home with children while wives earn a living, this scene could well be reversed.

Crises threaten marriage. By the very energy a crisis generates, however, it may be easier to cope with it than to survive the monotony of boredom. Remember the chapter on sharing activities? Perhaps now you can see even more clearly why a good marriage requires such creative ideas and their follow-through.

In some marriages the wife is responsible for filling the social calendar. In others, the husband does that function. I have learned that each hopes the other will enter into the fun-planning for both. To avoid boredom, you need to consider these ideas:

1. Once a week plan a spontaneous, impulsive activity. The word plan, of course, contradicts impulsive. And that's because you must be sure your time is free, the money is available, and, if you have children, that they are cared for. Still, the actual event may be a surprise. It could be a window-shopping spree without buying a thing —except maybe an ice cream cone at some point. A walk in the park or a hike on your bikes on the weekend are other inexpensive ideas.

2. Many communities are organizing a group of families who commit to trading baby-sitting on designated evenings. Child care can become less a problem if you can work out a similar plan.

3. You don't have to go out to have fun, and at some point children can even add to it. Play games, develop a mutual hobby, plan some home improvements, work out a budget that will afford a bit of saving for a special goal. (Obviously, the latter must be done carefully, or you will fight!)

Boredom does not need to threaten your marriage. But do remember this: when an exciting-looking detour appears in the person of a flirtatious "other," run for your life. Such a detour is usually deadly. Stick with your marriage vows—be committed.

Disagreements

It is often reported that most marital disagreements occur over money, sex, or children. The order of these three varies, but count on it. One of these three will be part of your arguments in some way most of the time.

Kent was an insatiable stamp collector. He read history and was well-informed about quality, rarity, and prices. Everyone needs a hobby, so why were Kent's philatelic activities a problem? The simple answer was that he spent too much money. Polly, his wife, went without many of the items she needed and wanted because he could not resist the temptation to enlarge his expensive collection. She developed a growing resentment toward him and his stamps. She wanted out of her marriage, believing that Kent's collection had become a jealous mistress competing with her for his love.

All relationships involve disagreements, but when they become intense and are unrelenting they threaten a marriage. This threat can be avoided. Think about these methods:

1. *Agree together about boundaries.* Discuss the amount of money and time you can each afford to give to a selfish interest. Hopefully, each of you will give in some, and you can reach a fair compromise. If not, you may very well need the help of a counselor or mediator.

2. *Stick closely to the concept of what is right and good for both of you.* Do not argue from a stance of proving you are right or manipulating to get your way. If either does so, the negotiations will fail.

3. *Review your marriage vows.* If all of us knew what would be included in the simple wedding vows made so innocently in a few blissful moments, we might back out entirely. It is in the area of major disagreements that those vows must return to focus. "For better, for worse, for richer, for poorer, in sickness and in health . . . till death do us part," were the words repeated by a handsome young couple only last evening. The "worseness" of basic disagreements will challenge most marriages, so renew those vows daily.

4. *Practice the discipline of self-denial.* This means *both* of you. Polly was too giving and enabled Kent to pursue his interests unchecked. Certainly at times she asked him to moderate his spending, but she had no idea how to be firm in setting boundaries and keeping within them. She had to learn to say, "No more services until you con-

sider me a partner." You must define for yourself what "services" mean, but you must be concise, firm, and follow through. Kent had to learn self-denial and some common-sense limits in his spending.

5. *Learn how to disagree without becoming disagreeable.* If you are clear about your information, open-minded in listening to the other's facts, and fair and reasonable about making decisions, you can settle any difference harmoniously. You can stay committed.

Disillusionment

When I was in college, a classmate told me this funny story: A ministerial candidate was searching for a wife. He had no end of candidates but finally narrowed his choice to one of two women. One was gorgeous but with no talents that would enhance her role as a clergyman's wife. The other was downright ugly, but she sang like an angel. The man finally chose the singer, believing she would bless his congregation.

The couple got through the courtship and the wedding and went off on their honeymoon. The morning after their wedding night dawned brightly, and the groom awoke early, gazing at his new bride. He cried out desperately, "Honey, please wake up and sing to me!"

In today's culture, people get to know each other very well before marriage. But even so, there is a period of disenchantment. He has halitosis in the morning and leaves dirty socks on the floor. She has premenstrual syndrome and takes so long getting dressed they are usually late. These small issues are only annoying and rarely cause divorce, but they threaten the commitment, creating barriers of resentment.

Recently a mother and her four children gathered in my office. Her husband and their father had become so abusive they were physically unsafe with him. They had to leave home. This man had seemed to be the ideal husband at first. He was socially charming, earned a good income, and helped make their home a showplace. But he had a short anger-fuse and a violent temper. He was not safe to be around, and the family found protection in a shelter.

Usually the disenchantment is not so extreme and life-threatening. More commonly, it is connected with his getting fat or her careless housekeeping habits. She felt he would do anything in the world to please her, but he wouldn't cut the grass when it became shaggy.

How do we deal with the disillusionments in marriage? What can compensate for those distortions or absent qualities we were so certain would not be a problem—but they are? Can we ever change one another? It's so tempting to try! Here are some answers:

1. *Define and discuss the dreams each of you have for your marriage.* The home you develop, the activities you want to share, the security you hope to accumulate, the trips you plan to take, the children you'd like to raise are examples of dreams many couples share. Do everything you can to bring these dreams to life. Make them happen when you can. But be realistic. Some of them won't materialize.

2. *Give up the dreams that are impossible.* My husband will always prefer museums and books to mountains and ocean sunsets. Without even realizing it, I spent precious years trying to teach him to love my things—nature, farms, birds, and animals. He has tried, but they are simply not woven into the fiber of his being as they are in mine. Giving up my dream that he would stand in awe for hours seeing and hearing the ocean waves beating against that rocky Maine coast was a painful loss. I grieved over it.

3. *Understand and work your way through your loss.* Despite your best efforts, whatever you have dreamed for your marriage may not happen. And when a dream dies, you will feel a poignant grief, similar to the feeling you

know when a loved one dies. Just endure that. Earlier we thought about the patient endurance that is required to build strong character. Endurance will also see you through the process of grief over the loss of some of your dreams. This grief will pass.

4. *When you have finished your grief, move on to enriching the good parts of your relationship.* Ask yourself now: What are the goals and dreams we can honestly share? How can I help make these materialize?

5. *Think commitment.* When you have worked your way through your disappointment, recovered from your grief, and accepted your reality and actual possibilities, you will be ready to build. And what you can build will be based not on a fantasy but on the honesty of unconditional love.

Sadly enough, many marriages weakly survive on false dreams or pretense. "You are not all I hoped you were. I don't like some of your habits and disagree with a few of your values. But I will pretend they are OK and make myself believe you are different from who you really are." That is not healthy love.

Remember 1 Cor. 13? Love believes *all* things—not just the good. And it keeps on loving. Love hopes all things, discovering some of those hopes will be dashed. It still keeps on loving. It endures all things even when endurance is indescribably painful. It keeps on loving. That is commitment.

Commitment demands tough love at times. Tough love establishes boundaries between who I am and who you are. When these boundaries are clear, you will not become an enabler of one another's weaknesses or faults. You will see clearly what problems exist and to whom they belong. But you will not assume the responsibility for fixing them when in truth you can't fix them. They belong to your spouse. When the problem is yours, hopefully you will find solutions. You will always help and encourage each other in the growth and change you choose to take on.

Tough love may say to your partner, "Dear, what you did is not worthy of you. You are bright, kind, and efficient. I'm sure you'll not repeat this mistake. Would you like me to remind you if I promise not to nag?" Obviously you need not memorize my words, but perhaps they will inspire some of your own answers toward issues in your marriage that need to be corrected.

Let me remind you of the power of forgiveness and its regular application. You must acknowledge the pain your spouse, knowingly or not, may inflict. You will need to spend some time finding out why he or she did that painful act. You must be willing to let go of the memory of it all. You will need to allow your information to become profound understanding. You must keep clearly in mind that such pain is not to be inflicted again and determine what each of you must do to prevent that. Finally, by an act of your will, you must choose to relinquish all anger or bitterness.

I cannot emphasize enough the importance of refusing to bring up past events. When your spouse does slip and repeat hurtful acts at times (with his or her being only human, that is likely to happen), deal only with the here and now. Adamantly refuse to bring up the past. Loving commitment allows the use of old mistakes only to build a better present and plan more wisely the future you may be given.

Summary

In building your healthy marriage, let's review what you must do:

⁓1. *Acknowledge, express, and enjoy your sexuality.* Remember: God created Eve for Adam as a partner and taught them to live together in joy and love.

2. *Build strong self-esteem in order to avoid the crippling blows of jealousy.* An inferiority complex makes both partners vulnerable to many problems.

3. *Order your own priorities.* Others may recommend their value order, but no two families are alike. Honoring God first and your spouse second gives you plenty of freedom for other needs.

4. *Develop strong spiritual bonds, which are crucial to healthy living.* You must be individually committed to Christ, but the best marriages grow on the mutual sharing of faith in Him.

5. *Keep a positive, affirming atmosphere in your home so you can enjoy marriage.* Practicing the art of patience, kindness, and good humor creates exactly that climate.

6. *Communicate effectively.* This is a skill most people must learn. Even when such lessons are laborious, endure them. Countless battles and immeasurable pain will be prevented when you know how to listen sensitively, read body language accurately, and speak understandably.

7. *Understand that each person is endowed with a set of inborn personality traits.* While these may be modified, it is impossible to change them totally. And it is unfair to ask or expect one another to do so.

8. *Practice interdependence.* By the time people marry, they have developed some degree of independence. Finding the balance in dependency and interdependency is no easy task, but you can do it. Learning to balance each other's strengths and weaknesses in a loving way is interdependence—vital in a healthy marriage.

9. *Build a strong character.* This is easier if you were blessed with parents who cultivated that. Many people today are not so blessed. If you are unfortunately one of them, begin now. Build with God's help the character He wants for you. The four cardinal virtues can help you learn how to create a godly character.

10. *Commit yourself fully.* The crown of a healthy marriage must be commitment. This quality requires self-denial, wisdom, patience, and immense determination. It is a quality that will weave strength and purpose into your life and make your marriage a unique masterpiece.

Building a marriage is not a happening. It is not easy and may present seemingly insurmountable difficulties. With God's strength, love, wisdom, and righteousness, you can do it. It's the first step in framing better families.

Reflection and Action

Commitment, especially in relationships and marriages, may be on the wane in Western society. Ketterman believes there are six pillars of strength on which healthy marriages and families may be built.

1. Dr. Ketterman lists the six pillars of strength in this chapter. Review this list and select one word for each pillar that sums of the core meaning of each pillar:

   a.

   b.

   c.

   d.

e.

f.

2. One threat to commitment is the combination of crises and loss. In the text, Ketterman writes of balancing idealism and reality. Reflect on these questions and respond.

   a. Why do some mates place their spouses on a pedestal?

   _____

   _____

   _____

   b. In your opinion, why are so many marriages hurt by the occurrence of an affair? _____

   _____

   _____

   c. What are some reasons for declining moral values and personal character in our society? _____

   _____

   _____

3. List three *impulsive* things you have done recently:

   a.

   b.

   c.

4. How do you deal with boredom?

5. The following is a two-part exercise: First, list the central issue

   in the last disagreement with your spouse _____

   _____

   Ketterman lists the following principles, which have been
   summarized for convenience, for dealing with disagreements:

   a. Boundaries (give and take)

   b. Justice (what's right)

   c. Faithfulness (promise-keeping)

   d. Self-denial (putting another first)

   e. Reasonableness (open-minded)

   Take the central issue identified in part one, and apply the five
   principles above. How would the application of these principles
   affect the disagreement?